MW01283687

DECODING SPANISH WINE:
A BEGINNER'S GUIDE TO THE HIGH-VALUE, WORLD-CLASS WINES OF SPAIN

By Andrew Cullen and Ryan McNally

Book design by Karrie Gawron

Cover design by John Yardley

Copyright © 2018 by Andrew Cullen and Ryan McNally

TABLE OF CONTENTS

Chapter 5: Primary Spanish Wine Regions (Denominaciones de Origen)..................... 37

CHAPTER 1: LA INTRODUCCIÓN

When it comes to wine, most fans are on an endless search to find an awesome value. After all, who doesn't like sampling an $8 bottle that tastes like it costs $15, a $15 bottle that sips like it set you back $25, or a $30 bottle with the depth and mouthfeel of a $50 beauty? Enter the world of Spanish wines.

Of course, there's much more to Spain than a good wine bargain. You've got amazing art and architecture, pulsing nightlife that stretches into the wee hours of the night – and frequently the early hours of the morning – and delectable dishes (paella, anyone?).

So whether you're traveling to Spain and want to learn more about the culture, searching for good values and have heard that Spanish wines are some of the best, or looking to stretch your wine knowledge beyond California, France and Italy, Spanish wines make fantastic additions to your wine exploration.

INTO THE WORLD OF SPANISH WINES

When you think about the world's top wine regions, what comes to mind? Bordeaux, Burgundy, Tuscany and perhaps Napa? You rarely hear people say Priorat or Ribera del Duero – at least not yet. But there's a good case that these regions, and a few others in Spain, should be on that list.

Remember Malbec 10 years ago? You'd be lucky to find three or four bottles at your local wine shop. Now there are entire sections dedicated to it – and we expect the same to happen with some of Spain's key regions.

Many mainstream wine buyers know little about Tempranillo (and even less about Mencía and Monastrell), but we think red wine fans who love Malbec, Cabernet Sauvignon or Syrah might thoroughly enjoy these varietals, if only they tried them in all their glorious forms.

Wine drinkers are always looking for great wines at great prices. And these bottles do exist, but they can be tough to find – especially if you don't know what you're looking for.

That's a challenge we aim to address with this book – to explore the wines of Spain, where some of the world's highest-quality, best-value wines can be found right now. We want you to discover what many adventurous wine drinkers have already found: a treasure trove of awesome wines that possess unique characteristics representative of the Spanish terroir and are a ton of fun to enjoy with friends and family.

THE DECODING WINE BOOK SERIES

Writing this book on Spanish wine is part of our ongoing effort with the "Decoding Wine" series to take the potentially intimidating process of learning about a wine region and make it fun and approachable. That means covering a country's key varietals and wine-growing regions in a conversational style and mixing in cultural tidbits and fast facts in a guide that's easy to understand – and hopefully a lot of fun to read.

Andrew started this series with a short pocketbook titled "Decoding French Wine: A Beginner's Guide to Enjoying the Fruits of the French Terroir" that found an audience with emerging wine lovers. That led to the collaboration with Ryan on "Decoding Italian Wine: A Beginner's Guide to Enjoying the Grapes, Regions, Practices and Culture of the 'Land of Wine,'" which was a more in-depth look at Italian wine but one that still aimed for a fun, non-snobby, easily accessible feel.

Along the way we've connected with tons of readers who share our interest and enthusiasm for trying new wines and experiencing new cultures. So here we go again, tackling another major wine-growing region.

OUR EXPERTISE IS IN NOT BEING EXPERTS

So who are we, and why are we experts on Spanish wine now too?

Truth is, we have no formal training. But we think that works to our advantage because we're like you: interested in exploring and learning about wine, but not wanting to be inhibited or bogged down by fancy wine terms and confusing jargon. We want to find bottles to enjoy by understanding what's available, the geography and story behind the wines, and the culture surrounding them, and then begin to build an informed profile that fits our palate.

Like most of you, we also don't have thousands of dollars to spend every month on fancy wines that Parker rated 94-plus points. Instead, we might have less than a hundred bucks (sometimes much less), and we want to get enough wine to keep our bellies full and smiles on our faces – and the faces of those enjoying wines with us. We wholeheartedly believe that's possible with proper exploration.

Ultimately, that's what's brought us to the wines of Spain: quality + value + style.

WHAT WE HOPE YOU TAKE AWAY FROM READING THIS

Our goal is that by the end of reading this book, you can understand Spanish wines in almost any setting and find wines you know you'll enjoy. This includes opening up the wine list at a Spanish restaurant and not feeling as though it's written in a different language (even if it is mostly in Spanish). Instead, your eyes will automatically pick up key cues: regions you know, grapes you prefer, vintages you know were good and producers you enjoy. Rather than being intimidated, you'll feel informed, confident and excited – and darned thirsty.

Same goes for when you visit your wine retailer. You'll be able to effortlessly browse the selection – red, white and sparkling – knowing the nuances of what the various wines offer and honing in on the best buys for your taste.

CHAPTER 1: LA INTRODUCCIÓN

Another side benefit: When you attend a dinner party, you'll have the knowledge to bring over the most interesting bottle of wine and have paid the least for it compared to other partygoers. That's always our objective. It's not easy, but it's a fun goal. And Spanish wine will help you achieve it.

SPECS

Now that we've explained what we hope you'll get out of this book, let's share a little more about us.

Name: Andrew Cullen

Things I do: Digital marketer, founder of CostcoWineBlog.com, author and co-author of three nonfiction books about wine and two fiction novels, *The Callisto Symphony* (2015) and *A Gentle Slaughter of the Perfect Kind* (2017)

Twitter: @CostcoWine, @AndrewsGuide

Websites: www.CostcoWineBlog.com, www.TheUnderSide.com

Spanish red wine I'd recommend: La Rioja Alta Gran Reserva 904 ($40 at Costco, several vintages available, all good, but the older the better for this one, see if you can find 2001)

Spanish white wine I'd recommend: Cabaleiro Do Val Albariño (2013 vintage available now, $27 from www.WineLibrary.com, one of my favorites from Rías Baixas, renowned winemaker)

Favorite Spanish restaurant: Jaleo in Washington DC

Favorite Spanish wine region: Tough call, but I'd go with Priorat

PAGE 9

Name: Ryan McNally

Things I do: Digital marketer, founder of VivaItalianMovies.com, connoisseur of heavy metal music

Twitter: @VivaItalyMovies

Websites: www.VivaItalianMovies.com

Spanish red wine I'd recommend: Tabula Ribera del Duero (several vintages available, 2012 was $29 from www.WineLibrary.com but currently sold out)

Spanish white wine I'd recommend: Antxiola Getariako Txakolina (2016 vintage available now, $15 from www.WineLibrary.com)

Favorite Spaniards: Salvador Dalí (past), Pedro Almodóvar (present)

Favorite Spanish wine region: Ribera Del Duero at the moment

LET THE GAMES BEGIN

So let's get into it. Remember that learning about wine is also a study in geography, which is especially true for wines from Spain as well as France and Italy. Spain's not a huge country, but every pocket will have different wine-growing methods, climates and soil (terroir), so the styles will vary.

As we've said many times, learning about wine requires exploration. Be adventurous. Try new wines, even ones that might not sound appealing to you in this book, because you never know what you might think. That's how you build a palate for wine, and we hope that reading this helps you in your journey. *Salud!*

CHAPTER 2:
SPANISH WINE HISTORY AND CURRENT CULTURAL OVERVIEW

The intersection of Spanish wine with the country's history, geography and culture gives it its own unique identity. Let's take a look at what you should know about Spain's background and heritage as you're kicking back with a tasty Tempranillo.

THE SIGNIFICANCE OF OLD WORLD WINES IN A NEW WORLD

Recently, Andrew was fortunate enough to try his second bottle of First Growth French Bordeaux, a 1995 Chateau Latour. As you may know, the five First Growth Bordeaux estates produce some of the most prized and expensive wine in the world, and an opportunity to enjoy a bottle doesn't come around that often for most wine drinkers.

It opened up closed at first, light and delicate, lacking discernible fruit, then moved into more of a graphite/magnesium phase. Eventually, it transformed from a dusty barnyard into an elegant, beautiful wine with aromas jumping out of the glass and a multidimensional fruit profile and finish that lasted for hours (or so it seemed).

Why are we sharing this with you? Because it was the utmost expression of Old World wine elegance and perfection. If your wine drinking has been centered on New World areas, such as the United States, New Zealand, South Africa and Australia, you've probably begun building a palate around big, heavy, dense wines that are fruit forward with punch-you-in-the-face intensity.

While we're fans of many of these wines, Old World wines from France, Italy and Spain offer a different approach. There's a history to their winemaking craft, a tradition perfected over centuries and across multiple generations. There's also a culture where these wines play a pivotal role.

After tasting that 1995 Latour, it became clear why European winemakers and consumers might be skeptical of high-end, expensive New World wines. Comparing the 20-year-old Latour to a 20-year-old Joseph Phelps Insignia from Napa (another of our favorite wines) is like comparing a Rolls Royce to a Lamborghini. Both awesome cars, but two very different executions.

So, as we begin our dive into Spanish wine, it's important to realize that it's an Old World wine-growing region. In fact, it's one of the oldest. That's not to say there aren't a few producers making New World-style wines, because there are, and many of them are very good. But to build a knowledge bank about Spanish wine, it's imperative to learn about its history and appreciate the heritage of Spanish winemaking that brought us to where we are today.

FAST FACT

Spain is the third-largest producer of wine in the world behind Italy and France.

A BRIEF HISTORY OF SPANISH WINE

Wine has been made in Spain for at least the last 3,000 years, and according to some reports, grapes could have been grown in Spain as far back as 4000 B.C. The Phoenicians planted early grapes in the Sherry region after arriving around 1100 B.C.

The Romans later helped accelerate winemaking's growth in the region as they were consuming and trading wines throughout their empire. At that time, wine production became the main source of prosperity for most of the country's population, with many of the Spanish wines being exported regarded among the highest quality in the Roman Empire.

With the arrival of Islamic rulers (the Moors) in 711 A.D. after the fall of the Roman Empire, wine commerce was put on hold due to the Moors' religious beliefs prohibiting alcohol consumption. Although most production halted, the Moors did keep select vines dedicated to growing wine grapes, particularly those used to make the popular fortified wine Sherry, which was then (and is still) one of the most popular Spanish wine exports. This lasted until the defeat of the

Moors in 1492, at which point Spaniards regained control of their country and planted new vines, breathing life back into the Spanish wine trade.

In the mid-1800s, the phylloxera epidemic that killed most of Bordeaux's major vines led to many of that region's winemakers coming to Spain to continue making world-class wine without the uncertainty of what would happen to French vines. This was an important turning point in Spanish wine history, as the top knowledge and talent – the winemaking all-stars at the time – began influencing the burgeoning Spanish wine trade, which would benefit from their insight and experience.

During this era, Spanish winemakers learned about maturing grapes longer on the vines, how to blend red and white grapes, and how to properly barrel age the wines to create rich, full, complete wines worthy of aging and standing on the global stage next to the most highly regarded wines in the world.

In the late 1970s, following the death of long-time dictator Francisco Franco, Spain transitioned to democracy. Combined with other related factors, such as Spain's joining the European Union in 1986 and adopting the Euro in the early 2000s, this democratic era has driven strong economic growth that has helped Spain's wine market flourish. And that's where it is today.

FAST FACT Wine was among the provisions Christopher Columbus requested for his voyage to the "New World" in a letter to King Ferdinand and Queen Isabella.

WEATHER, GEOGRAPHY AND GRAPE GROWING IN SPAIN

Spain's long wine history has provided winemakers with a track record for what works and what doesn't for growing grapes across the country. And that's a good thing, because Spain is unique geographically, a peninsula that has multiple elevations and weather patterns throughout the land.

The central part of Spain, for example, can get super warm in the summer and colder in the winter. In fact, areas like Andalucía in the southcentral part of the country can reach 100 degrees Fahrenheit in the summer, making them more suitable for fortified and dessert wines.

The northwest part of Spain, on the other hand, has ocean breezes and rivers. The Mediterranean side also has warm temperatures and cooling breezes. Meanwhile, the southern portion of the country is drier with strong winds, providing a less-than-stellar climate for grape growing.

In most of Spain's top wine-growing areas, the climate is ideal with warm days and cool nights. Many of the vineyards are above sea level, with several rising as high as 3,000 feet. Some mountain vineyards go even higher than that.

In Chapter 6, we'll take an in-depth look at Spanish wine classifications. As you'll learn, during the last century Spain has built a system for organizing the wine trade based on several factors, including geography, the types of grapes grown in particular areas, and the winemaking practices and traditions of the various regions.

Much of this is based on the rich history of Spanish winemaking, the years of testing and tasting, and the tireless efforts of generations of winemakers working to perfect their craft. We're fortunate to live when we do, not only because we have easy access to these wines, but because we literally get to enjoy the fruits of centuries of labor.

THE CURRENT STATE OF SPANISH WINE AND CULTURE

Making sweeping generalizations about a country can be dicey, especially in today's fast-changing world, but it's safe to say wine is deeply woven into the fabric of Spanish culture. As in Italy and France, Spain has seen a decrease in wine consumption in recent decades, but it remains an integral part of the country's DNA, especially at mealtime.

Lunch is the most important meal in most parts of Spain, a lengthier and later affair than we're used to stateside. It often includes three courses and typically takes place sometime between 1 p.m. and 4 p.m. A typical "comida" might kick off with a soup or salad, move on to a larger meat or seafood-based dish, and then conclude with a small dessert.

As with many other European countries, mealtime is a leisurely event with plenty of time to savor your food and drink and enjoy good company. If you're eating out, this extra time can also be used to corral your waiter, a task roughly as challenging as returning a Rafael Nadal forehand.

Enjoying a glass or two of wine is the norm at these meals, with red more commonly consumed unless you're in a region that specializes in white.

If you're feeling sleepy at the thought of a big lunch accompanied by a few glasses of vino, welcome to one of Spain's most glorious contributions to modern civilization: siesta. That's right, the Spanish tradition of a mid-afternoon time block dedicated to resting and napping provides the perfect way to beat the heat and recharge for an evening of revelry. Even with pesky legal and cultural shifts chipping away at its length, siesta remains prevalent in most of Spain, though larger cities such as Barcelona and Madrid sometimes break from tradition in this regard.

Moving into evening, wine drinking becomes more of a wild card, with beer and mixed drinks increasingly entering the fray and consumption based more on personal preference than cultural norms. The grazing period prior to dinner is a popular time for drinking wine and enjoying tapas, and you'll also see some Spaniards imbibing in vino at dinner (typically taking place between 8 p.m. and 11 p.m.) and, of course, into the late hours of the night.

Given the surge in tapas' popularity outside Spain, it's understandable if you're a little burned out on the concept. Still, should you be fortunate enough to travel to Spain, you must experience the thrill

FAST FACT

Spanish painter Salvador Dalí's 1977 wine book *Wines of Gala* features sections on "Wines of Aestheticism," "Wines of Sensuality" and "Wines of the Impossible." While we won't cover these deliciously offbeat topics in this book, we appreciate the maestro's willingness to tackle them.

of walking into a Spanish bar or restaurant, ordering a glass of wine, and enjoying the local specialty served up with a tapa (frequently olives for the first round and delectable house specialties afterwards). More often than not, it will be a phenomenal wine you've never tasted.

Many of these wines aren't exported, but never fear: Today you can find more Spanish wines outside the home country than ever. With that in mind, let's start learning about the grapes and regions that create all those delicious wines around Spain.

CHAPTER 3:
MAP OF KEY SPANISH WINE REGIONS

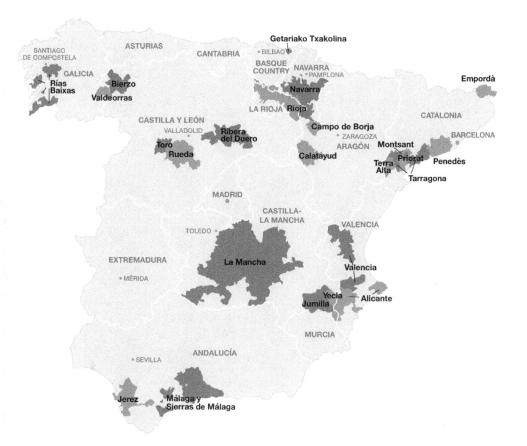

CHAPTER 4:
PRIMARY SPANISH GRAPE VARIETALS

Grapes are a key starting point to decoding Spanish wine. In addition to many popular varietals that you'll find grown all over the world, Spain is home to many native varietals that are delicious as well. Believe it or not, Spain has more land dedicated to growing grapes than any other country. There's a lot to learn here, and we don't attempt to cover it all in this book.

Instead, we aim to arm you with knowledge of the primary varietals you can reasonably expect to find at restaurants and wine shops near you. You'll learn what to anticipate from the various winemaking styles and taste profiles of these grapes across different regions of the country.

It may surprise you that Spain, by volume, produces more white grapes than red. When we talk about Spain as a strong value location for finding amazing buys, that most certainly includes the country's white wines, many of which feature varietals that aren't the center of discussion in grocery store wine aisles.

That's part of the reason you should try these wines, and many of the other varietals we'll cover in this section. In wine, the underdog grapes often provide the best value. Let's look at the key varietals of Spain and see if we can find some newcomers worth seeking out.

KEY WHITE GRAPE VARIETALS

ALBARIÑO

Albariño ("ahl-bah-reen-yo") is one of the easier-to-find Spanish white wines that we'll look at, and also one of the best values. Today, more restaurants are featuring Albariños, presumably because they pair well with a wide variety of foods, and wine shops are carrying them in greater abundance to reflect growing consumer demand and interest in the varietal.

Generally priced under $25 and often closer to $12 – particularly if you browse the selection at Costco or Trader Joe's – Albariño is a real crowd pleaser. It should satisfy almost any white wine drinker, from Sauvignon Blanc to Chardonnay fans, even though it's a different style of wine.

This varietal is grown in the far northwestern corner of Spain (about 10:00 if you want to overlay a clock on a map of the country), so it's right on the edge of the coast, allowing the grapes to benefit from a cool sea breeze. The primary area within Spain for many of the Albariños you'll find for sale in the United States is Rías Baixas, which we'll cover in more depth in the next chapter looking at Spanish wine regions.

Albariño is typically very bright and crisp, perfect for warm weather enjoyment. It often pours a medium yellow in the glass and tends to have a good body and heft to it, especially compared to thinner Sauvignon Blancs or other light white wines. Albariño flavors are usually lemon, lime, apricot and peach with some tart and citrus. You also get a fair amount of acidity that can be dialed up or down based on different winemaking styles.

Major Albariño wines that you'll commonly see in the United States include Martin Codax, Nora, Kentia and Burgans, all of which we've enjoyed on countless occasions.

FAST FACT

Albariño is also grown just over the border in Portugal, where it's labeled as Alvarinho. A few years back Andrew purchased a bottle of Alvarinho thinking it was Spanish Albariño, but the mistake turned out to be a blessing in disguise as the wine was excellent and tasted just like – wait for it! – a very nice Spanish Albariño.

VERDEJO

Some wine drinkers feel whites are bland and uninteresting. Fair enough. But if an endless parade of generic whites has soured you to their appeal, you might want to try Verdejo ("vehr-DAY-hoh"), an interesting grape grown in Spain's Rueda region.

Verdejo dates to the 11th century, but it's seen a surge in popularity in the last decade or two. In the right hands, these grapes can produce wines with a most outstanding combination of fruit and acidity. You'll typically get some wild herbs and fruit on the nose, with flavors including melon, apple and stone fruits. Rounding out the package is some mineral character, as well as notable acidity that balances out the flavor and helps make this a very food-friendly wine.

Speaking of which, seafood of all types, chicken and saltier foods should pair well with Verdejo. Bottles will typically run $10 to $15, with the occasional outlier going a little higher or lower.

Verdejo is sometimes blended with other grapes, and while this can often yield fantastic wines, we recommend you try some straight-up Verdejo to fully immerse yourself in the experience. You won't be disappointed.

FAST FACT

Spanish actress Penélope Cruz contributed label artwork for the 2012 Vicente Gandia "Whatever It Takes" Verdejo, with proceeds going to various charitable causes.

GODELLO

How you like them apples? Godello ("goh-DAY-yoh"), a grape found in "Green Spain" regions such as Valdeorras, Ribeira Sacra, Bierzo and Ribeiro, typically produces medium-bodied whites with flavors of apple, along with citrus, pear, melon and peach depending on the bottle.

Godello is often likened to Chardonnay, minus the heavy oak and butter flavors found in some U.S. versions, but that's really not doing this grape and its aromatic wines justice. In addition to the fruits mentioned above, Godello will often exhibit some stone, minerals and maybe even white pepper on the finish, along with a crisp acidity that makes Godello a stellar wine for pairing with seafood, cheese, roast chicken and the like.

These whites will typically set you back a little more coin, often starting around $18 and running up into the $30s, but we've found they usually justify their higher price point.

MACABEO (ALSO KNOWN AS VIURA)

Macabeo ("mah-kah-BAY-oh") is a grape you'll likely come across in your Spanish wine exploration, and one you should definitely try. It's really the Swiss Army knife of versatility for Spanish white grapes, a hard-working varietal that's excellent across many different styles of wine, from sparkling to dry to sweet.

Macabeo is the primary grape used to make white Rioja, which you might not expect since most people think of big, powerful red wines when they think of Rioja. Surprise! Rioja has a softer, gentler side, with excellent white wines and even rosés.

Macabeo is often used as a blending component for both red and white wines and can take on different styles and flavors depending on how it's employed. For instance, Macabeo is utilized in Penedès to make sparkling Cava, a much different use for the grape than in the white wines of Rioja.

XAREL·LO

Those floral aromas, citrusy flavors and fresh acidity you love so much about Cava? You can thank Xarel·lo ("shah-REHL-oh") for helping out with those. Commonly grown in Penedès in the northeast corner of Spain near France, Xarel·lo is most likely to turn up when you're cracking some Spanish bubbly.

On rare occasions you may come across a single varietal Xarel·lo (oaked or unoaked), which can range from medium and fruity to full-bodied with more of a mineral finish depending on the winemaker

PARELLADA

One of the "Big 3" grapes typically found in most Cavas, Parellada ("par-eh-YAH-dah") also helps contribute the flowery fragrances and citrus-y flavors you'll usually find in a bottle of Spain's bubbly. It's mostly grown in the Penedès region, which occasionally churns out non-sparkling whites featuring Parellada, but these are rarely exported.

PALOMINO

Palomino ("pahl-oh-MEE-noh"), which is also known as Listán or Jerez, is one of the primary three grape varietals used in the production of Sherry. They are thin-skinned grapes with low acidity and are better known for their vibrant aromas than their robust flavor, which is why they're ideal for making Sherry.

AIRÉN

Even as a fledgling wine enthusiast, you likely know the most popular wine grape varietals: Cabernet Sauvignon, Merlot, Tempranillo, Chardonnay, Syrah and … Airén?

That's right, Airén ("i-RHEEN") trails only Cabernet Sauvignon and Merlot as the most widely planted grape in the world. It's the big dog in the La Mancha region of central Spain, with hundreds of thousands of acres dedicated to growing it.

So why haven't you heard of Airén? For starters, its primary use is for making brandy. And when it comes to wine, it's known more for its ability to withstand the region's inhospitable climate than for the delicious bottles it yields.

Some Airén is used for blending, and you'll occasionally see it exported as a single varietal offering. When done well, these are dry, light, crisp whites that are often available at bargain prices, but they remain tough to find stateside.

TREIXADURA

Treixadura ("treh-shah-DOO-rah") is a common blending varietal found in Spain and Portugal and worth noting because it's often used with Albariño and the aforementioned Alvarinho in Portugal to add extra body and aromatics.

KEY RED GRAPE VARIETALS

TEMPRANILLO (ALSO KNOWN AS TINTO FINO, CENCIBEL AND ULL DE LLEBRE)

Tempranillo ("tem-prah-NEE-yoh") is the second most widely planted grape overall in Spain (behind Airén) but it remains the most heavily planted red varietal. More importantly, it's cemented its place as Spain's flagship red grape – and the world has taken notice. Tempranillo, and wines made from Tempranillo (it's not always listed front and center) dominate the Spanish sections on restaurant wine lists and in wine shops.

This is in part because of growing consumer interest and the food-friendly nature of these wines, but also because for straight bang for the buck, almost any Tempranillo will compete with bottles from other countries that cost two or three times as much. Sure, that's a generalization, but we feel these wines offer some of the best values in the world today, and we think you'll agree.

Tempranillo is a thick-skinned grape that produces wines with moderate tannins that benefit particularly well from oak barrel influence. To this extent, Tempranillo is fresh, vibrant and enjoyable in its youth, while still retaining the structure and depth to mature into an even finer wine with additional barrel and bottle aging.

Many of Spain's most prestigious red wines, including those from Rioja and Ribera del Duero, include a majority of Tempranillo in their blends.

Among winemakers, Tempranillo is known as "little early one" because it ripens earlier than Garnacha.

GARNACHA

Don't call it a comeback! With apologies to LL Cool J, Garnacha ("gahr-NAH-cha") has been here for years, and it's currently the third most planted red grape in Spain. But it's gone through many ups and downs, including phases in which yield was high and quality low, and others during which it was primarily used as a blending component.

Today, especially in the regions of Calatayud and Priorat, it's being given attention as a varietal that stands on its own, and the result has yielded some outstanding wines that can often be found at bargain prices.

You might know Garnacha (or Garnacha Tinta, to distinguish it from its white Garnacha Blanca sibling) by its French name Grenache (grown primarily in Southern France) or even its Italian moniker Cannonau (usually found in southern Italy or Sardinia). But while Garnacha is one of the 10 most-planted varietals in the world, it originated in Spain, where it's well suited for the hot, dry, windy conditions prevalent in the Mediterranean valleys.

On the nose, you'll frequently get dark cherry aromas, with more of that as you drink along with some dark berry and plum flavors.

Toasty, fleshy and big on the palate, Garnacha often finishes spicy with a dash of pepper. As you might expect based on this description, Garnacha will typically pair well with beef and lamb, spicy/dark sauces and pastas with red sauces.

Depending on the region, you may get a stronger minerality or oakiness element mixed in. And speaking of geography, other key Garnacha areas include Campo de Borja, Montsant, Cariñena and Somontano, though these are a little tougher to find outside Spain. Garnacha is also grown a good amount in Rioja, where it's often used as a blending component for the region's famous Tempranillo.

MONASTRELL (ALSO KNOWN AS MOURVÈDRE)

Monastrell ("maw-nah-STREHL") is a sweeter, tannic red grape, so sweet in fact that it was once used to make dessert wines. But now, winemakers have discovered its potential to make truly great, powerful, dry reds that are fruity yet balanced, structured and elegant.

The varietal is popular in southeastern regions such as Valencia, Jumilla, Alicante and Yecla. Given its late ripening and high yield, Monastrell wines can usually be scored at a fraction of the price of some of Spain's other popular reds (usually under $15), making them an easy choice for you on your Spanish wine journey.

MENCÍA

As dry and dusty as one of the Sergio Leone spaghetti westerns filmed in Spain – and with plenty of the intensity and brooding spiciness of those movies as well – Mencía ("men-THEE-ah") is a grape you don't want to miss. Most often grown in the northwestern Spain regions of Bierzo, Ribeiro and Ribeira Sacra (as well as Portugal), it's sometimes likened to Cabernet Franc.

Mencía will often deliver some flowers and dark berries on the nose, with flavors of dark cherry. At their best, these wines are earthy and tannic yet balanced, pairing well with steak, pork and stews. Prices usually start around $15 and rise steadily from there.

CARIÑENA (ALSO KNOWN AS MAZUELO, CARIGNAN)

Cariñena ("car-eeh-YEHN-ah") is one of Spain's most widely planted grapes and is often used as a blending component due to its frequent high acidity and strong tannic structure. The grape produces wines that are robust and balanced, with Garnacha and Syrah making up its most common blending "friends." When used in a blend, Cariñena can soften and balance wines while adding a rich black and berry fruit layer and enhanced aromatics.

Cariñena is primarily grown in the autonomous communities of Catalonia and La Rioja, although other regions also use the grape in their wines. Many of Spain's most popular and prestigious wines include Cariñena in their blends, including wines from Montsant and Priorat.

GRACIANO

Graciano ("grah-thee-YAH-no") is a black-skinned red grape that's grown in the Navarra and Rioja regions of Spain. This hard-to-grow, low-yielding varietal is well known for its ability to age, in barrel and bottle, to produce wines that may be tight and young at first, but have the structure to develop into some of the most prized wines in Spain, including the amazing Gran Reserva wines from Rioja, which are among our favorite Spanish wines.

The grape produces wines with intense aromas and rich color, along with vanilla and spices.

BOBAL

Given that it's the second most widely planted red grape in Spain (trailing only Tempranillo) and has a funny, memorable moniker, you might be surprised that you've never heard of this one, but there are a couple of reasons for Bobal's ("boh-BAL") relative obscurity.

First, it's rarely exported stateside, though that's slowly showing signs of changing. Secondly, it's typically been known as more of a blending grape. However, there are a couple of regions aiming for Bobal stand-alone success, including Valencia and Utiel-Requena, a region in east-central Spain where Bobal comprises more than 80 percent of the area's production.

The skin of the Bobal grape has a large quantity of anthocyanins, the fancy term for the compounds you probably know and love for giving red wine its pigmentation and antioxidant power. So there's plenty of dark color and intensity in your average Bobal, as well as a high level of tannins that can lead to a rich drinking experience – or a rather harsh, unpleasant one. With the good bottles, you'll usually get dark berry aromas with plum and spice flavors and perhaps some chocolate and toastiness to round out the experience.

Even in a limited sampling, we've experienced a wide range of price points and quality in Bobals. Proceed cautiously but have fun experimenting – you might land a wine with complexity and intensity that far exceeds its price tag.

GARNACHA TINTORERA (ALSO KNOWN AS ALICANTE, ALICANTE BOUSCHET)

Garnacha Tintorera ("gahr-NAH-cha tin-toh-rare-ah") is a deeply colored, thick-skinned red varietal that has the rather uncommon distinction of having colored juice as well as color in the skins. This makes Garnacha Tintorera an interesting blending component, and while it's not a wine you're going to see on your average wine list, it's an old-world varietal that's worth noting.

MATURANA TINTA

Maturana Tinta ("mah-too-RAAH-nah TIN-tah") once held an important spot among Rioja's top varietals, but over the years a combination of disease and the rising favorability of other varietals has led to its near-extinction.

However, recently the grape has been receiving more attention in Rioja, even being allowed back into the red wines of Rioja, and time will tell if this rare grape is able to stage a late-in-life comeback. This is probably a varietal you'll have an easier time finding in Spain than anywhere else, so make a note on your next trip to see if you can find it.

CHAPTER 5:
PRIMARY SPANISH WINE REGIONS (DENOMINACIONES DE ORIGEN)

A study of geography may not sound very appealing when, to quote Thomas Haden Church in the oenophile favorite *Sideways*, the most important wine question on your mind is *"When do we drink it?"*

Still, broadening your understanding of Spain's wine regions is an important aspect of enjoying the country's wine – and trust us, a lot of fun too. As we discussed in Chapter 2, Spain boasts a wide range of climates, landscapes and cultural traditions. In many cases, these translate to fiercely localized wines, and it's part of the reason decoding Spanish wine means building a basic understanding of Spanish geography.

This can be a daunting task for newcomers unfamiliar with Spain. The country is made up of 17 autonomous communities, and among these areas are 69 DO regions (see Chapter 6 for more classification info) that you'll see on wine labels, each with its own unique history and characteristics. To add to the chaos, you'll find that wine websites, stores and restaurants sometimes slice and dice Spain's wine regions in different ways.

If this sounds more painful than a razor blade to the eye a-la Luis Buñuel's silent classic *Un Chien Andalou*, don't you fret. In this chapter, we zero in on the 25 DO regions you're most likely to find as you're trying new Spanish wines. Plus, we've organized these regions into five directional areas that provide a sense of location without demanding a detailed knowledge of Spanish geography.

The goal is to keep it entertaining while providing a manageable amount of info that will entice rather than overwhelm. Let's get into (wine-drinking) character.

NORTHCENTRAL SPAIN

RIOJA

Rioja ("ree-OH-hah") is the powerhouse Spanish wine region, well known for its Tempranillo-based red wines. The area's wine growing dates to the Roman era, but things really exploded when the phylloxera outbreak destroyed many French vines, and those winemakers headed to nearby Rioja to continue their world-class winemaking (as mentioned in the Spanish wine history section).

Rioja's wine cultivation is separated into three regions: Rioja Alavesa, Rioja Alta and Rioja Baja. The first two have rather similar continental climates, while the latter boasts a warmer, drier, Mediterranean-influenced climate. Rioja's landscape is shaped by seven major rivers that bring plenty of water to the area.

Rioja wines are made primarily with Tempranillo, with smaller parts of Garnacha and maybe some Graciano and Mazuelo. Rioja Blanco is typically made with Macabeo, with smaller portions of Malvasia and Garnacha Blanco.

There's a heavy French influence in Rioja winemaking, and the region's wines generally see a great deal of oak influence, with the wines aged for several years before being released to the public. As we cover in the "Classifications" chapter, Rioja wines can fall into one of four categories depending on how long they've been aged: standard Rioja, Crianza, Reserva or Gran Reserva.

FAST FACT

Some Rioja vineyards are actually listed in adjacent Navarra, but the wine produced from those vineyards is counted as belonging to Rioja.

RIBERA DEL DUERO

Most fledgling Spanish wine drinkers think "Rioja Tempranillo" when it comes to Spanish wine. But like Pamplona bulls nipping at the heels of runners, Ribera del Duero ("ree-BEH-rah dehl DWEH-roh") has been coming up hard behind Rioja as the premiere Spanish wine region. The area boasts its own complex, tasty version of Tempranillo – often called Tinto Fino – to rival Rioja and is now home to more than 200 wineries.

Located about two hours northwest of Madrid, Ribera del Duero packs some blistering heat in the summer and some serious cold in winter, while rainfall is low to moderate, with the occasional fierce hailstorm thrown in for good measure. Rocky terrain, heavy plateaus (most vineyards are situated well above sea level, which also helps mitigate the harsh daytime temps) and the Duero River (the third largest in Spain) round out the landscape.

It may not sound like the best place for creating awesome wines, but the Tempranillo grape is ideally suited for the climate, boasting thick skin and typically ripening before the summer heat blazes at full force. And the 50- to 60-degree swings between day and night? No prob, the wildly fluctuating temperatures are said to give the grapes structure and character.

Enough about the terroir, what about the wines? Ribera del Duero's Tempranillos generally boast blackberry aromas, flavors of fruit, rich tannins and medium to high acidity. Starting around $12 and running way up from there, these are flavorful, complex wines that are super food-friendly and provide excellent value (for now), often drinking like wines twice the dollar amount.

As with Rioja, Ribera del Duero wines are often classified by age, which we cover in Chapter 6. Given their complexity, they may still benefit from airing out for a while if they taste too closed after opening.

These wines will pair well with equally powerful foods such as roasted meats, rich pork dishes, cured hams and flavorful sharp cheeses. If you want to go hardcore, you could fire up some lechazo asado, a roast suckling lamb dish popular in the region.

What about other grapes? Whites are pretty non-existent, save for some Albillo here and there. There are a few other red varietals grown here – notably Cabernet Sauvignon, Merlot, Malbec and Garnacha Tinta – but these are primarily used for blending. Mostly, it's all about the Tinto Fino, which led *Wine Enthusiast* to name Ribera del Duero its 2012 Wine Region of the Year.

FAST FACT

At the Baños de Valdearados, a small pueblo in the center of Ribera del Duero, there's a 66-meter mosaic tile floor dedicated to Bacchus, the Roman God of wine and debauchery. It's believed to date back more than 2,000 years.

RUEDA

This region shares a few commonalties with Ribera del Duero, its neighbor to the east. For starters, the Duero River snakes through each. Both experience hot summers, cold winters, and sizeable temperature swings between daytime and night. And each has a climate seemingly perfectly suited for its key grape.

That's where the similarities end, at least as far as wines go. While Ribera del Duero is all about red, it's the whites that matter in Rueda, especially the local Verdejo.

Although Rueda ("roo-EH-dah") doesn't have a huge presence outside its home country – but look for that to change soon – its wines are actually the most-consumed white wines in Spain. The Verdejo grape has been grown in Rueda for more than a millennium but has had its ups and downs over the years, barely avoiding extinction around 100 years ago but rebounding strong as the 20th century wore on, with Rueda achieving DO status in 1980.

Verdejo is flourishing there now, with those generous day-night temperate fluctuations believed to provide just the right balance between sweetness and acidity. Get your hands on a bottle and you'll see what the fuss is about, with the wines often packed with the type of flavor and complexity that make the typical $10 to $15 price tag look like quite the bargain. (For more, check out the Verdejo section in the "Grapes" chapter.)

Bottles with the Rueda Verdejo designation require at least 85 percent Verdejo, with the local Viura grape or Sauvignon Blanc often comprising the rest of the blend. If you just see the Rueda designation on the front label (without Verdejo), this indicates a minimum of 50 percent Verdejo. Located roughly 100 miles northwest of Madrid, Rueda is definitely a Spanish wine region to keep on your radar.

TORO

In the northwestern part of Spain, just 40 miles from the Portugal border, is Toro ("Bull"), a wine-growing area that's rapidly rising in popularity as more wine consumers discover the amazing wines and almost ridiculously low prices for which they can acquire these wines in the United States.

FAST FACT

In the 13th century, King Alfonso IX of Leon famously said – referring to the symbol of the Bull for Toro and the lion as the Kingdom of Leon – "tengo un Toro que me da vino y un León que me lo bebe." Translation? "I have a bull who gives me wine and a lion who drinks it."

Toro, which is located on a high plateau in the autonomous region of Castilla y León, has a continental climate with low rainfall, warm temperatures and chilly winters. Toro is best known for its Tinta de Toro, the local name for Tempranillo, which comprises much of the red wine produced, alongside Malvasia Blanca and Verdejo, which is used in Toro Blanco on the white side.

NAVARRA

Navarra, located just north of Rioja, is a lesser-known wine region but a well-known area since it's the home of the annual Running of the Bulls (Sanfermines). It's an area we see gaining momentum, with more bottles popping up around our local wine shops and even at big-box stores like Costco.

Navarra wines are typically not very expensive (often under $15), but they are nicely assembled, flavor-packed, fruit-forward wines that hardly seem to match the price you pay for them – you'll likely guess they cost much more.

This small region generally sees hot, dry summers and cooler winters, but that climate can vary across its diverse landscape. The area is impacted by the surrounding Bay of Biscay, the lower hills of Pyrenees and the Ebro River basin, as well as the many elevation changes throughout the landscape.

Like many of the regions we've discussed, Navarra is predominantly planted with red grapes, including Tempranillo, Garnacha, Merlot, Cabernet Sauvignon, Mazuela and Graciano, while white grapes include Garnacha Blanca, Chardonnay and Viura. At one point it was well known for its rosé wines made from Garnacha, but now it's become more popular for its dry reds.

FAST FACT

Chapter 15 of Ernest Hemingway's *The Sun Also Rises*, set in Pamplona during the Running of the Bulls, contains more than two dozen references to wine.

CALATAYUD

Looking for a region that combines that enticing Spanish mix of delicious wines and strong value? Enter Calatayud ("kah-lah-tah-yood"), an area in northcentral/east Spain that's producing some super-hot Garnacha right now – for some extremely reasonable prices.

Yep, we're talking high-quality juice for $10 to $15, and sometimes even less. Mostly reds, with white varietals making up less than 10 percent of the region's yield. Of the reds, Garnacha is by far the most prevalent, with production outnumbering runner-up Tempranillo by more than 6-to-1.

About an hour's high-speed train ride from Madrid, Calatayud has a couple of interesting geographic features that lend the area to outstanding Garnacha. Start with big differences in temperatures between day and night, toss in some high-altitude mountainous slopes, and mix in a bunch of different soils, and you've got a terroir in which the Garnacha grape thrives.

The aromas and tastes of Garnacha are covered in detail in the "Grapes" chapter, but when it comes to sampling Garnacha from Calatayud, keep in mind that the soil in the area where it's grown can impact style. Some sub-regions will deliver wines exhibiting more minerality and spices in their aromas, while soil in other areas will yield wine with greater fruitiness. Taste a few and see what you dig.

CAMPO DE BORJA

Campo de Borja certainly doesn't sound like the easiest place to grow wine when you consider its arid, unpredictable climate, but winemaking here dates to the Cistercian Monks in the late 12th century. Today, Campo de Borja (cahm-poe day BORE-ha) produces many excellent, moderately priced wines that are becoming more readily available across the United States, and we find them to be quite delicious. Rainfall is light in this part of Spain, and the temperature varies significantly, but many of the higher-elevation old vines around Campo de Borja, some of which are almost 50 years old, are known to produce excellent Garnacha, albeit in relatively small yields.

The soil of Campo de Borja plays a big role in the style of wines produced here. Much of the area is planted in soil with brown limestone and stone deposits that are rich in iron and lime and provide excellent natural drainage.

FAST FACT

The "Cierzo" is a wind that blows cold, dry air down from the northwest through Campo de Borja, contributing to its climate but also occasionally damaging the vines due to the sometimes harsh gusts.

More than half of Campo de Borja is allotted to Garnacha, which thrives here, followed by Tempranillo. The rest of the grapes produced locally are also generally red, including Mazuela, Merlot, Syrah and Cabernet Sauvignon.

GETARIAKO TXAKOLINA

Part of the fun of travel is the sense of adventure and opportunity to experience something new, and that's true with wine too. Well, prepare to have some serious fun when sampling Txakoli, the key wine from Getariako Txakolina ("get-tahr-eeh-yah-koh chok-oh-LEEN-yah") that's as fiercely independent as the Basque region it hails from in Northern Spain.

For starters, the name. It looks more Greek than Spanish, right? Basque Country (País Vasco) has its own language and culture, with the "Tx" forming a "Cha" sound. The weather? Cool and damp, with annual rainfall the highest of any Spanish wine region. Not exactly your prototypical wine-growing climate, but the native Hondarrabi Zuri grape used for Txakoli thrives here (along with neighboring Arabako Txakolina and Bizkaiko Txakolina).

Before you even sample it, Txakoli ("chok-oh-lee"), offers some fun options. Sure, the classic wine glass works for this white wine, but in its home region it's often served in tall tumbler or cider glasses, so feel free to grab a similarly shaped receptacle. Txakoli is a little "jumpy" – more on that later – so if you're feeling wild, make like a Basque bartender and tame that beast by pouring it from a foot (or more) above your glass.

Ready to drink? The fun continues with a beguiling mix of green apple and citrus flavors, just the right amount of acidity and a dash of sparkle. The carbonation comes from Txakoli's unique winemaking process: It's left to rest on the "lees" (the residual yeast), giving it some spritz when it comes out of the bottle.

This refreshing wine is perfect for warmer weather or if you want to loosen up a stodgy wine-tasting gathering. As you'd expect from a wine hailing from Basque Country, an area known for its mouth-watering cuisine (see: San Sebastian) and experienced fishermen, Txakoli will pair well with seafood – especially anchovies if that's your thing.

Bottles typically run $15 to $20. It's still a bit tough to find Txakoli outside Spain, but that's changing quickly: exports to the United States increased tenfold from 2000 to 2010. You might even find a rosé version here and there. Grab a bottle, work on your Basque high pour, and let us know how it goes. *Topa!*

NORTHWEST SPAIN

RÍAS BAIXAS

A pint of Albariño for ya, eh? OK, so you'll never hear these words uttered in Rías Baixas ("REE-ahs BYE-shas"), but you may hear some bagpipes, and given our Irish heritage we appreciate this region's Celtic links – as well as its delicious Albariño wines.

The climate and landscape here evoke Ireland's frequent rains, mist-covered houses and castles, green fields and rocky coasts versus the prototypical drier Spain with its endless plains. Rías Baixas is part of the autonomous community of Galicia ("Green Spain"), and its locale is a perfect fit for the region's Albariño grape.

A whopping 99 percent of Rías Baixas wines are whites, with 90 percent of those Albariño. You'll get some variance in Albariño through Rías Biaxas' five subregions – taste and compare, we beg of ye – but most will boast aromas of apple, butterscotch and melon giving way to flavors of pear, honey, apple and almond and a long, balanced finish. (For more, check out the "Albariño" section in the "Grapes" chapter.)

What's the secret to banging out such tasty wine despite the wettest, coolest, lushest climate in Spain? While the factors are many, a few stand out, starting with the high level of minerality in Rías Baixas' soil, which makes its way into the local wine. Second, the winemakers employ a few savvy tactics to combat the rain, such as using a wine trellis called a "parra" to ensure that the vine height and spacing allow for greater air circulation, even ripening and an absence of mildew.

Extended contact between the yeast lees (sedimentation that's left after fermentation) and the wine, a technique used in Rías Baixas and a few other regions of Spain, provides additional character. And despite the overall rain, there's enough sunlight to build up some good acidity, although yields are generally low.

Add it all up and you've got some crisp, charismatic white whites that are rising in popularity and absolutely worth your time. Try pairing Albariño with some seafood – fishing is huge in Rías Baixas and these wines are a perfect match – or enjoy it solo while the sounds of "la gaita" (the traditional regional instrument, a.k.a. bagpipes) play in the background.

FAST FACT

Local legend says that during creation God rested for a moment in Galicia, and the Rías Baixas are the traces left by the fingers of God's hand.

VALDEORRAS

Valdeorras ("val-day-OH-rahs") is becoming one of the emerging areas for white wine in Spain and is beginning to attract more attention in the global wine community. Located 90 miles inland and along the River Sil, the climate in the Valdeorras region is wet with plenty of sunlight and heat in the summer that create lush, green backdrops, but temperatures can get quite cold during the winter months.

The popular white grape grown in Valdeorras is Godello, which has made a comeback since being replaced in the '70s by Palomino. Godello, which typically offers citrus fruit flavor, herbs and mineral notes with healthy acidity and sometimes a touch of spice, is unique among Spanish whites in that it can be aged to evolve into something grander. To that extent some in the wine world have referred to Godello as the "white Burgundy of Spain," which is saying a lot for the quality and potential for these wines.

Other, more obscure white varietals found in Valdeorras include Palomino, Doña Branca and Lado. For reds, you'll find wines that are rich and fruity made from Garnacha, Mencía and Gran Negro along with other local varietals.

Overall, Valdeorras is a region that's growing in popularity, driven by high-quality white wines that are beginning to attract attention, so it's definitely an area to keep an eye on.

BIERZO

This region is a stopping point on the Camino de Santiago (St. James Way), an important Christian pilgrimage during the Middle Ages, but you'll have to decide whether quaffing Bierzo's wines qualifies as a religious experience.

Much of that will depend on your affinity for Mencía, the grape that makes up about 75 percent of Bierzo's production and is rarely grown outside this region. Located in northwestern Spain, Bierzo ("bee-EHR-thoh") has a more moderate climate than some of its neighboring regions, with the Sierra de los Ancares mountain range providing a barrier from the Atlantic Ocean.

Other key grapes here include Palomino (used for Sherry and blending) and Godello, which comprises a mere 4 percent of Bierzo's grape growth but seems to pop up a decent amount on U.S. wine shelves.

FAST FACT

Bierzo is home to Las Médulas, built 2,000 years ago and the most important gold mine in the Roman Empire. Today, tourists from around the globe visit to take in the stunning landscapes, and UNESCO has declared Las Médulas a World Heritage Site.

Still, Mencía is the driving force behind Bierzo's rapid popularity growth, with the region's milder temperatures and sponge-like soil believed to contribute to its wines' lushness and big mouthfeel.

Botillo, a sausage-like pork dish that reigns as one of Bierzo's signature food items, makes a perfect pairing with Mencía. Check it out if you're fortunate enough to visit the area.

NORTHEAST SPAIN

PRIORAT

Priorat ("pree-oh-RAHT") has more than 5,000 acres of vineyards across its hilly landscape and has established itself as one of the wine world's most important and prestigious growing areas. But like most wines from Spain, Priorat wines, while not inexpensive, are generally priced very competitively against their high-end counterparts. We'd put a $60 Priorat wine up against many $100 to $150 bottles from other countries in a blind test any day.

Priorat produces big, bold wines that benefit from the Mediterranean climate, and they can be blended from a wide range of different grapes or styles given the hilly terrain that allows vineyards to plant, and benefit from, grapes grown at high and low elevations. This puts much of the art of the wine in the hands of winemakers who must blend the grapes together to create an expressive, terroir-driven wine that's elegant and complex.

Priorat's history involves many acclaimed French winemakers coming to the region following the phylloxera devastation in the late 1800s that wiped out numerous French vineyards. These newcomers to the area brought with them many fine winemaking techniques along with grapes such as Cabernet Sauvignon, Syrah and Merlot. These grapes are now found alongside Cariñena and Garnacha in the blends of wines of Priorat.

PENEDÈS

Located along the Mediterranean coast in the autonomous region of Catalonia, Penedès ("pehn-eh-DESS") has a long winemaking history and is the birthplace of Spain's famous sparkling wine, Cava. Barcelona, located just 30 minutes away, serves as a major hub for the bustling wine activity of the surrounding area.

Grapes grown in Penedès benefit from a warm, mild Mediterranean climate that cools down in the nearby foothills and sees moderate rainfall. The soils are rich with limestone and clay. Xarel·lo is the most widely planted varietal here, with much of that going into Cava. While much less widely exported, Penedès also produces some non-bubbly, Xarel·lo-based wines that are typically dry, fruity and medium-bodied with good acidity.

FAST FACT

Ninety-five percent of Spanish Cava production takes place in the Penedès region

MONTSANT

Montsant ("moon-sahn") is an important area to check out, as it seem more and more bottles from here are showing up in wine shops and on wine lists. It's kind of like what Côtes du Rhône is in relation to Châteauneuf-du-Pape in France, a lesser-known region than its more famous neighbor, Priorat, but one that kicks out amazing wines at unbeatable prices. Montsant wines are usually made from Garnacha, Carignan and Syrah on the red side, and Garnacha Blanca on the white side.

Can Blau is a popular Montsant producer whose wines are readily available nationwide, some starting around $10.

TERRA ALTA

Terra Alta (the "Highlands') is another winemaking part of the wider autonomous Catalonia community that reaches an elevation of 3,000 feet. Similar red blends are produced here, but they remain relatively out of the mainstream wine spotlight right now, which helps create competitively priced bottles that are worth putting on your radar.

The most popular red grapes grown in Terra Alta are Garnacha and Carignan, followed by Tempranillo, Cabernet Sauvignon and Merlot. On the white side, you'll find Garnacha Blanca, as well as Parellada and Macabeo, which are used to make Cava.

EMPORDÀ

Empordà is a wine-growing region in the northeastern corner of Spain and an area that receives plenty of moisture from the nearby Mediterranean. On the flip side, though, strong winds flow through the area that help reduce exposure for mildew that might creep up. The area was originally known for its rosè wines, but these now account for only about 17 percent of Empordà's wine production as its reds have grown in popularity due to their full body and complexity.

The reds are comprised of mainstay varietals like Cabernet Sauvignon, Merlot and Syrah along with Garnacha, Tempranillo, Carignan and Mourvèdre. White Garnacha is popular on the white wine side as well as Macabeo, Chardonnay, Muscat and Xarel·lo.

The area also makes dessert wines that are favorites of the locals. Some of these are made from Garnacha, while others are assembled by blending lesser-known local varietals.

Although Empordà is one of the world's oldest wine-growing regions, it's still relatively under the radar of many consumers, so you can score high-quality wines from this area at great prices. That makes it another one to remember in your Spanish wine exploration.

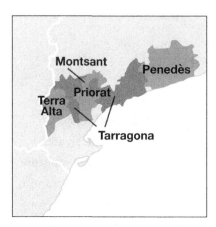

TARRAGONA

Located in Northeast Spain, immediately west of Penedès and a short train ride from Barcelona, Tarragona ("tah-rah-GO-nah") is another region to keep an eye on. Though still sparsely exported, you may find some Tempranillo (known locally as Ull de Llebre) and red blends (common grapes include Garnacha, Merlot, and Cabernet Sauvignon) from Tarragona online or at your local wine store. Macabeo, Parellada and Xarel·lo are also grown here, with many of these grapes heading over to Penedès for Cava production.

SOUTHEAST SPAIN

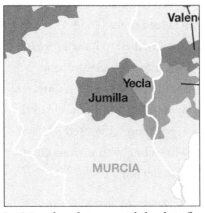

JUMILLA

Feeling parched? Welcome to Jumilla ("hoo-MEE-yah"), a region of scant rains but rich, full-bodied wines, mostly of the Monastrell variety. Located in the southeast of Spain, Jumilla is flanked by the Mediterranean Levante coast and the Castilla La Mancha plateau, with both influencing the area's climate.

Dryness is the most notable aspect of that climate, but never fear: Monastrell has adapted quite well and represents more than 80 percent of the region's production. These are typically dark-colored, big-bodied reds with notable tannins and spice. (For more, see the "Monastrell" section in the "Grapes" chapter.)

Reds make up more than 95 percent of the wines here, with other varietals including Cencibel (the local name for Tempranillo), Garnacha, Cabernet Sauvignon and Syrah, some of which you'll occasionally see blended with Monastrell.

If you like wines with a little heft, Jumilla offers some strong values, with rich and tasty Monastrells often running in the $10 to $15 range.

ALICANTE

Talk about history – King Louis XIV of France (1638-1715) was documented to have a love for Alicante wine that he took to his deathbed, while as Queen of Spain Elisabeth Farnese (1692-1766) reportedly used Alicante wine along with various culinary delights to bend Spanish King Philip V to her will.

So how's the region faring 300 years later? Like its neighbor Jumilla, Alicante ("ah-leeh-CAHN-tay") is known for its hot, dry climate and equally intense Monastrell wines. Shop around and you can get some stellar buys in the $10 to $20 range that exhibit the classic dark fruit flavors and toasty finishes of Monastrell.

Monastrell makes up 75 percent of the vines grown in Alicante and is easily the most exported grape, though the region also produces hardy Spanish varietals such as Garnacha Tintorera, Garnacha and Bobal, along with Syrah, Merlot, Cabernet, Pinot Noir and Petit Verdot. Muscat, a light white with aromas of flowers and orange balanced with a touch of acidity, is the region's primary white.

If you're looking for a totally unique drinking experience, keep an eye out for Alicante's Fondillón wine. Made from over-ripened Monastrell grapes, put through a complex barrel-aging process and tough to find outside Spain, this dessert wine (a perfect match for dark chocolate) often delivers an enticing mix of dry and sweet. Think nuts and dried fruit, with some leather and tobacco creeping in with age. Prices usually run $40 and up.

Finally, if you like to munch on nuts while sipping some vino, Alicante is one of the primary sources of Marcona almonds, a sweeter, fatter and rounder variant of the California version you're probably used to and a fine match for the aforementioned Fondillón (or Sherry).

In Alexandre Dumas' literary classic *The Count of Montecristo*, the count offers Major Cavalcanti a glass of Sherry, Port or Alicante. The major chooses Alicante, declaring it his favorite wine, and when the count serves up a perfectly aged bottle and biscuits, it helps pave the way for a productive meeting.

YECLA

Another popular Mediterranean-bordering wine region is Yecla, which happens to also rank among the smallest of Spain's wine regions. And that's surprising because wines from Yecla can be found rather easily at many U.S. restaurants and wine markets.

Why the disparity between production volume and accessibility? For starters, 85 percent of the wine produced in Yecla is exported. In addition, local heavy hitter Bodegas Castaño has made a concerted effort to vault the region onto the international stage. As a result, you can readily find, learn about and enjoy these great wines.

Monastrell is the most popular wine from Yecla, although you'll find other Spanish varietals here like Garnacha Tinta and Garnacha Tintorera, along with some of the more common varietals such as Cabernet Sauvignon, Merlot and Syrah. Monastrell from Yecla has grown in recent years to become more complex and cellar-capable, and like most Spanish wines, Yecla wines remain inexpensive for the most part.

On the "Yecla Blanco" white side, you'll find Airén, Merseguera, Chardonnay and Macabeo, along with a few rosés.

FAST FACT Yecla represents just one half of one percent of the total plantings in Spain and is home to just 11 wineries.

VALENCIA

Valencia, as many know, is Spain's third largest city and is situated near the middle of the eastern coast of Spain. The area is popular for its white sandy beaches and vibrant nightlife, but it's also an important part of Spain's wine world. In addition to producing increasingly higher-quality wines in the vineyards around the city, Valencia is the chief area in the country for exporting Spanish wines.

The climate differs across the various wine regions that make up Valencia, but it's primarily Mediterranean-influenced with hot summers and cold winters.

Moscatel is a popular dessert wine from Valencia and is made from the grape that shares its name. Across other areas of Valencia you'll find reds made from Tempranillo, Bobal, Mazuelo and Monastrell and whites made from Merseguera, Malvasia, Macabeo, Chardonnay and Sémillon, to name a few.

SOUTHCENTRAL SPAIN

LA MANCHA

"But is it not strange, Signor squire, that I should have so great and natural an instinct in the business of knowing wines, this let me but smell to any, I hit upon the country, the kind, the flavor, how long it will keep, how many changes it will undergo, with all other circumstances appertaining to the wine?"

– Miguel de Cervantes, "Don Quixote"

You don't have to be Johnny Depp to get lost in La Mancha, but navigating the vast region's wines can be as adventurous and occasionally disorienting as director Terry Gilliam found La Mancha during his failed attempt to film a Depp-starring Don Quixote movie there.

Located about an hour south of Madrid, La Mancha is huge, according to many sources the largest wine region in the world, occupying an area of more than 30,000 square kilometers. There's a real grab bag of grapes grown here in decent quantity, including Spanish varietals such as Tempranillo, Garnacha, Monastrell, Bobal, Verdejo and Viura, along with Cabernet Sauvignon, Merlot, Sauvignon Blanc, Chardonnay and many, many others.

That doesn't mean it's easy wine-growing territory. "La Mancha" is likely derived from the Moorish "al-mansha," which translates to "dry land" or "parched earth." With scorching hot temperatures and little rain, La Mancha presents some challenges, which is part of the reason the most popular grape to grow here isn't any of the big names above but Airén, the white grape often used for brandy.

You'll see a lot of bottles with the Vino de la Tierra designation coming out of the area, including some intriguing blends that combine a handful of the region's many grape options. Quality will vary, but you can score some real gems here.

Given all these factors, La Mancha is definitely a wine wild card, but as a result you can find some astonishing values. Shop around and do some sampling and you'll discover incredible wines for under $15 and sometimes even less than $10.

For cheese fans, La Mancha also offers the allure of its local Manchego cheese. Regional Tempranillo, Cabernet Sauvignon and Verdejo all make enticing pairing options depending on your mood and taste.

"When life itself seems lunatic, who knows where madness lies?" asked Don Quixote. "Perhaps to be too practical is madness." When your wine-drinking habits are getting a bit predictable, bust out of your routine and get a little lost in La Mancha.

MÁLAGA AND SIERRAS DE MÁLAGA

With some of Spain's best beaches and lots of sun to spare, Málaga ("MAH-lah-gah") is a tantalizing vacation destination. It's also one of the world's oldest wine-producing regions and is best known for its fortified sweet wines made from the white varietals Moscatel and Pedro Ximénez

The Moscatel (also known as Muscat and Moscato) grape doesn't have the greatest reputation in some wine circles, but we're starting to see some very interesting dry Moscatel wines hitting U.S. stores from the Sierras de Málaga DO. These are fruity and flavorful, often boasting tastes of tropical fruit, melon, apple and/or orange, but delivering good balance and a soft, dry finish.

Typically priced from $12 to $18, you might be surprised how much you enjoy these dry moscatel wines – regardless of whether you're rocking an ocean view.

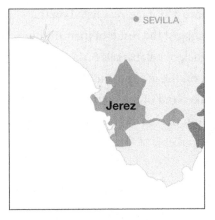

JEREZ-XÉRÈS-SHERRY

They say "there's a Sherry to suit every taste and occasion," yet this elixir remains a mystery to many wine drinkers. There's plenty of history around Sherry (the region and the beverage), from the Phoenicians bringing vines to the area in 1100 B.C. to 16th century explorers allegedly transporting the region's wines, making them the first to enter North America. But what do you need to know today?

The Jerez ("heh-REHS") region – also labeled Xérès ("heh-RETH") and/or Sherry – is located in the southcentral part of Spain, with the Guadalquivir River and the Coto Doñana nature reserve to the north. To the west you've got the Atlantic Ocean providing white sand beaches and cool breezes to combat the hot summer temperatures. Rainfall, heavier than in most of southern Spain, is captured in the region's albariza – limestone rich-soils – helping provide moisture for the area's grape vines.

Sherry is made from the Palomino grape and fortified after fermentation. Depending on the type, it can be aged under a layer of yeast known as the flor (which protects it from oxidizing), aged via the normal oxidation process (fortified to an alcohol level that prevents the flor's formation and allows the wine contact with air), or aged using a combination of the two processes. Color, aroma and taste can vary based on a myriad of factors.

Unlike most wines, Sherries don't have a vintage year listed on the bottle. Some kind of subterfuge? Nah, just the result of their unique solera blending process. Picture a stack of oak barrels (criaderas) with the oldest sherry in the barrels on the ground and the youngest up top. Every year some sherry is taken out of the bottom barrel to bottle. To refill it, sherry is added from the barrel level above it, and so on. This continues until the winemaker is at the top, at which time the latest year's vintage is added.

While the topic of Sherry could take up an entire book, that's likely beyond the scope of most fledgling Spanish wine drinkers. So, to help guide you through your tasting experience in a less intimidating fashion, check out the handy primer chart on the most popular types of Sherry on the next page:

	AGING PROCESS	COLOR RANGE	AROMAS	TASTING NOTES	SAMPLE PAIRINGS	OTHER NOTES
Manzanilla	Aged under veil de flor; produced only in bodegas of Sanlúcar de Barrameda	Bright, pale straw	Flowers, chamomile, almonds	Dry, fresh, vanilla, light acidity; dry, slightly bitter finish	Seafood, cured meats, olives	15-19% alcohol; serve very chilled. Price range: $9-$17+
Fino	Aged under veil de flor inside American oak casks	Bright straw yellow to pale gold	Almonds, wild herbs	Light, dry, delicate, apple, wild herbs, almonds	Tapas, olives, nuts, salty snacks, shellfish, fish	15-18% alcohol; serve chilled; good as an aperitif. Price range: $9-$18+
Amontillado	Unique dual process: First aged under the veil de flor, then exposed to oxidation post-flor	Pale topaz to amber, depending on aging time with flor versus oxidative	Caramel, hazelnut, herbs, tobacco	Balanced acidity, complex, medium-bodied, hint of sweetness, toffee, dry finish, nuts, mushrooms	Soups, white meat, wild mushrooms, artichokes, mild cheeses	16-22% alcohol; serve slightly chilled; can be stored open for months. Price range: $9-$20+
Oloroso	Added alcohol prevents veil of flor from forming, allows wine to age exposed to oxygen. Like Amontillado, can go decades in the barrel.	Rich amber to deep mahogany (longer aging = darker wine)	Toasted walnuts, balsamic, wood, tobacco, leather	Full-bodied, structured, powerful, smooth, caramel, fig, walnut, elegant dry finish	Red meat, stews, wild mushrooms, well-cured cheeses	17-22% alcohol; serve slightly chilled; can be stored open for months. Price range: $13-$25+
Palo Cortado	Produced from very fine must, fortified to 15% and aged in casks; then fortified to 17% to commence oxidative aging	Chestnut to mahogany	Citrus, butter	Deep, round; lingering finish. Think Amontillado nuance + Oloroso roundness.	Nuts, cured cheeses, stews, meats. Some prefer on its own.	17-22% alcohol; serve slightly chilled; can be stored open for months. Price range: $15-$25+

That's plenty to digest, but it's just the tip of the iceberg: In addition to the Fab Five, you can dig into sweeter Cream Sherries that may incorporate other grapes such as Moscatel and Pedro Ximénez and use concentrated rectified must (think of it as grape sugar) to add a touch of sweetness.

If cocktails are your thing, you can use Sherry as a mixer to complement gin (Manzanilla), whiskey (Amontillado) and other libations. It can also stand as its own foundation for mixed drinks, combining with stuff like vermouth, Cointreau and various bitters to form an array of light and exotic cocktails. Looking to spike some cider? Again, Sherry can fit the bill.

With Sherry's popularity surging and a massive array of tantalizing drinking possibilities, it's the perfect time to give these unique wines a sampling.

CHAPTER 6:
SPANISH WINE CLASSIFICATIONS

An integral aspect of "decoding" Spanish wines, in addition to evaluating the vintage, region and varietal, is understanding how wines are classified in Spain, along with related terminology designating the amount of time the wine has aged. In a forthcoming chapter (Chapter 9) about reading Spanish wine labels, we'll combine this knowledge so you can assemble all the clues on the label to know what to expect from the wine inside.

Let's first look at the Spanish classification system for wine, which is similar to what you find in other European wine-producing areas but very different than what you'll experience with U.S. wines. Wines in the United States aren't classified by a third party based on perceived quality of the producer, region of country and the vines. Across most of Europe, wines are classified this way, Spain included.

The goal of Spanish wine classifications is to give the buyer an indication of quality based on a subset of predetermined metrics, some of which carry more weight than others. But as you'll see, there are some high-quality areas of Spain that haven't achieved the top designation, so we'd advise you to take the classifications for what they are: a general guide and tool of knowledge to keep in the arsenal as you decode bottles.

Like any other wine region in Europe, there are wines classified at lower levels that many believe to be world-class, and wines classified higher that those same people don't acknowledge as superior quality. Ultimately, it's up to your individual tastes as a wine consumer. Having said that, you owe it to yourself and your wine studies to be educated, so that's what we intend to do here.

KEY CLASSIFICATION LEVELS

The first classification level for Spanish wines is simple and that is the table wine, or **Vino de Mesa**. From there, the next level is **Vino de la Tierra** (VdlT), which adds some additional geographic guarantees (the wine is from where it says it is) but is still rather loose with the winemaking methods.

For these basic wines, it's really not that important. They are what they are and they aren't trying to be anything more. We bet you'd be surprised, though, by how much you might enjoy some of these "table" wines. They are typically much higher quality than what we'd consider inexpensive table wines in the United States.

Next is **Denominación de Origen**, or DO, which includes 69 areas and is where a majority of Spain's wine resides. DO served as the upper echelon of the Spanish wine system until 1998, when the **Denominación de Origen Calificada** (DOC) level was introduced. Only two regions have earned DOC Status, Rioja and Priorat.

Then in 2003, one more level was added, **Vino de Pago** (VP), which indicates that the wine is single vineyard, estate grown. VP has been given to only 15 producers, and there's an inherent perceived level of quality associated with the moniker as well.

Again, these designations should serve as little more than a guide when researching wine. While we'd agree that Rioja and Priorat produce some of Spain's finest wines and should be labeled as such, you can find equally good wines (or maybe better depending on your preferences) from areas like Toro or Ribera Del Duero that are classified as DO.

One of the tricks to buying wine in France's Burgundy region is to find producers located next to the Premier or Grand Cru Chateaux, but who aren't labeled as such. These neighboring wineries share pretty much the same soil and climate as their famous (and more expensive) neighbors. They don't have the fancy designation, but often the wines are equally good. This is another reason why geography is so key to finding great wines.

So what do these wine classifications really mean? What purpose do they serve if two producers next to each other are classified differently? Some of the aspects of wine production that are governed under these designations include everything from what information is on the label to the types of grapes allowed to be grown and the amount of time required for aging the wines, which leads us to our next area of classification.

AGING DESIGNATIONS

Some Spanish wines, particularly those from Rioja, will have a one-word description on the label that pertains to how long the wine was aged prior to its release. This can include time in the barrel and the bottle, as determined by the winemaker by what will best benefit the wine.

Tinto/Roble/Joven: Wines with these designations have little to no oak influence and are released young, ready to drink.

Crianza: The wine has been aged for at least one year in oak and one year in the bottle.

Reserva: The wine has been aged for at least one year in oak and two years in the bottle.

Gran Reserva: These wines see extended oak aging of two years and three years in the bottle.

When you grab a bottle that's already been aged for you by the producer, it often isn't necessary to age it further. They've done all the work for you, in ideal conditions, so it's a nice way to enjoy older, more mature wines.

It's also worth noting that these aging designations apply primarily to red wines. Whites and rosés, which don't benefit as much from prolonged aging, are required to be aged for less time.

When you're browsing the Spanish wine aisle at your local retailer or perusing a list of Spanish wines at a restaurant, you'll likely come across these designations. When you do, you'll now know a little more about that wine inside. Experiment with Crianza and Gran Reserva bottles from all over Spain. See which ones you enjoy the most. Understanding the wine's sense of place and then knowing how it's been handled before arriving in your possession is a key to decoding Spanish wine.

CHAPTER 7:
SPANISH WINE VINTAGE REPORT

P art of what makes the wine game so fun (and challenging) is that in addition to learning about the many varietals and grape-growing regions, the ball is always moving to a new location through the different vintages of wine that are produced every year. Simply put, every wine is different every year, because as much as we'd like to say the wine is made in the barrel, it's really made in the vineyard through the terroir.

We recently heard an awesome definition of terroir that's fitting for this chapter: Terroir is "the sum total of all the elements that the winemaker is unable to control." A chief factor among those "elements" is the weather. Good fruit in means good fruit coming out, but it's hard to turn bad fruit into something great.

With that in mind, the vintage is something you should always take into account when buying wine. The good news is that neophytes don't have to memorize vintage charts for every region and year, but it's a wise idea to have a general understanding of years that were particularly bad or good.

Fortunately, there hasn't been a super-bad vintage for Spanish wine in some time, arguably since 2002, and before that maybe 1991, which we doubt you'll find hanging around at your local wine shop.

For the past decade-plus, Spain has seen average to above vintages, which makes buying Spanish wines that much easier. In short, there aren't a lot of alarm bells sounding on the vintage side. Still, there are a few nuances worth nothing, so let's dig in and take a look at the past 14 years.

2004-2005: Great vintages, and you're seeing some of the Reserva Rioja from these years in stores and restaurants. We find them to be drinking beautifully right now (2018).

2006-2007: Not bad, average overall, but there were some strange weather events that didn't help the crops, such as a hailstorm in Rioja and frost in Ribera del Duero.

2008-2010: All very good years for the most part throughout Spain. Temps were favorable in 2008, while 2009 was a little hotter but still produced great-quality wines. 2010 was close to perfect, the strongest of the trio, and a vintage to file away in your mind.

2011-2013: Good wine was produced during these years, which were about average, perhaps suffering from small weather bumps here and there, but for the most part nothing that should make you run for the hills. 2011 was hot but created some powerful wines, 2012 was dry and produced smaller yields, and 2013 was rather uneven, with a higher yield but unpredictable weather.

2014-2016: Still early for many of these wines, but they were incrementally better each year. Our advice? Just commit them to memory in order of appearance, with 2014 being more on the mediocre side, while 2016 might be the winner of the group. In short, 2014 was a step up from the previous year, and 2015 was a step up from there, albeit hot and dry, producing small fruit and lower yields, but delivering good juice. According to many sources 2016 was almost ideal with a huge harvest, so you'll want to keep an eye out for those to hit stores.

2017: This is going to be an interesting vintage to watch as conditions varied throughout the country (even frost up north), and it was one of the earliest harvests of all time. Reports indicate a lower yield and wines that exhibit more finesse than power.

As you progress in your journey with Spanish wines, try different vintages of the same wine and see if you can begin to tell the difference in the terroir year to year. With no recent years to avoid, you can safely buy vintages from the last decade, experiment at your leisure, and begin to learn about what styles and vintages you enjoy most.

CHAPTER 8:
TOP VALUE BUYS IN SPAIN –
10 BOTTLES TO LOOK FOR

We've now covered the major Spanish wine varietals and regions, and it's likely become clear that we feel, and many experts agree, that most areas of Spain offer incredible wine value and quality for the price.

In this chapter we'll highlight 10 easy-to-find bottles that exemplify this country's awesome wine values. These bottles are perfect starting points and representative of what you can expect from these areas and varietals as you explore further.

Of course, the vintages you'll find may vary (which is why we decided not to list current ones), but with a string of good vintages in Spain that – fingers crossed – will only continue, you should be fine with whatever year your local store carries.

We also want to encourage you (once again) to try new wines. When you were reading through our descriptions of the various varietals, some of them probably sounded more appealing to you than others. While your instincts will be correct in many cases, you'll likely also find that a few of the wines you thought you'd enjoy turn you off, while others that didn't sound as tasty rank among your favorites. The only way to know is to explore.

"Wine is similar to music in that it's a purely experiential realm, and it's a purely subjective practice. That's sort of the funny thing about wine criticism or, for that matter, music criticism. At times, those are useful guides, but ultimately it's all about how you react to that music or wine."

– Mike D of the Beastie Boys

Here's a good list of 10 top-value Spanish wines to start with:

1) Borsao Tinto
Hailing from Campo de Borja, this is full Garnacha for under $10 and a wine critic favorite, often duping blind tasters into believing it's a much more expensive bottle. With fresh fruit flavors and consistency from vintage to vintage, this is an excellent wine to taste as part of your journey, and if you agree with us, one that you might want to stock up on too.

2) Cune Crianza Rioja
This is an excellent buy in Rioja that you can find for between $12 and $15. We've even found it at Costco for only $11 a bottle, which is a steal. It's light in body but big on flavor, and Robert Parker frequently scores this wine in the 90s.

3) Evodia Old Vine Garnacha
This is a popular Spanish bottle from Calatayud that should be relatively easy to find. We've seen it just about everywhere we've

looked – even grocery stores and World Market. And the best part is that most places sell it for under $10, making it a strong value buy. This is signature Garnacha at an absolute steal of a price.

4) Can Blau Montsant

This is a red comprised of Mazuelo, Syrah and Garnacha that's also widely available. It's a good representation of the kinds of wines you can get from Montsant, and the price is only around $12.

5) Castaño Hécula Monastrell

This is a rather dry, tannic and young wine from Yecla with ripe fruit and a dusty finish, and a superb buy for only $7 (what else can you really enjoy for that price?). Stock up.

6) Burgans Albariño Rías Baixas

We're listing the Burgans because it's readily available nationwide, but be sure to experiment with a few different Albariños. This one can be scored for around $12 (though lately it seems to be edging closer to $15 as more people are turning on to the value of Spanish wine) and has just a touch of sweetness to the finish.

7) Lan Rioja Crianza

Another good buy from Rioja, this one is only about $11 and offers big cherry flavors with notes of vanilla and caramel. It's another pick that routinely scores 88 to 90 points among the critics.

8) Muga Blanco

A great white from a popular producer, this is an acidic wine with flavors of apple and pineapple. Blended from Macabeo and Malvasia, you should be able to find it for between $14 and $16.

9) Marqués de Cáceres Verdejo

Typically priced under $10, this Rueda white provides a budget-friendly intro to Verdejo, striking a good balance of fruit (apple, citrus) and acidity. Though you can naturally get better Verdejo upstream, this is an easy-drinking primer to the varietal and region that regularly shows up on "Top Value" lists.

10) Mercat Brut Nature Cava

No list would be complete without a great bubbly. You should be able to find this one for around $15. It boasts dominant flavors of apple, honeysuckle and apricot with a bit of acidity; overall it's super-refreshing.

And there you have it, a list of 10 great wines that you could purchase for a total of around $100. Combined with what you've read in this book, these wines will help shape your palate and provide a launching ground for discovering even more fantastic Spanish wines that you love.

CHAPTER 9:
READING A SPANISH WINE LABEL

Remember that confused look on Woody's face when Buzz Lightyear gets switched to "Spanish mode" in Toy Story 3 and starts speaking fluent Español? The same puzzled expression can be seen on many English-speaking wine fans as they browse the Spanish section at a wine shop. (We know, since we've worn a similar look of befuddlement.)

True, shopping for wine in a brick-and-mortar store has changed dramatically with the proliferation of smartphones. Once upon a time, you had to rely on your knowledge and, if you were lucky, a store employee's assistance to help you sleuth out the contents of a wine bottle. Today, you can pull out your phone, execute a quick search and usually get a detailed rundown of the bottle's contents, including critic and audience ratings.

Still, when you're in a store with hundreds of bottles of wine, you need a faster way to narrow your selection. Given the volume of choices and the myriad foreign languages on display, things can get overwhelming fast.

That's where the knowledge you've accrued in this book will come in handy. With some practice, you'll be able to quickly gauge what's in a bottle and how it syncs with your taste and what you're looking for. To help get you started, here are eight sample Spanish wine labels complete with descriptions of what the key elements of each label represent. Ready, set, shop!

1. **Winery name** (Bodegas)

2. **Appellation** (Region)
    We know Rioja will be predominantly Tempranillo.

3. **Appellation status** (Classification)

4. **Vintage** (Cosecha)

5. **Name of wine and aging designation**

6. **Producer and location**

7. **Bottle volume and alcohol %**

1. **Indicates grapes grown on property**

2. **Winery name** (Bodegas)

3. **Name they have given to this blend**

4. **Appellation** (Region)
   Again, we know Rioja will be predominantly Tempranillo.

5. **Appellation status** (Classification)

6. **Vintage** (Cosecha)

7. **Producer and location**

8. **Size and alcohol**

1. **Winery name** (Bodegas)

2. **Varietal makeup**
   (this label actually lists the blend)

3. **Vintage** (Cosecha)

4. **Appellation** (Region)

5. **Appellation status** (Classification)

6. **Producer and location**

7. **Bottle volume and alcohol %**

1. **Winery name** (Bodegas)

2. **Vintage** (Cosecha)

3. **Appellation** (Region)
    We know Toro will be predominantly Tempranillo.

4. **Appellation status** (Classification)

5. **Producer and location**

6. **Size and alcohol**

1. **Size and alcohol**

2. **Winery name** (Bodegas)

3. **Appellation status** (Classification)

4. **Appellation** (Region)

5. **Varietal**

   (This wine is predominantly Verdejo)

6. **Producer and location**

Other notes: Vintage is not listed on label, which means it's likely on the back label or the bottle's neck.

1. **Winery name** (Bodegas)

2. **Appellation** (Region)

3. **Appellation status** (Classification)

4. **A little bonus here** about the vineyard that translates to "the hillside slate vines"

5. **Size and alcohol**

Other notes: Again, the vintage isn't listed, which means it's likely on the back label or the bottle's neck.

1. **Vintage** (Cosecha)

2. **Name they have given this wine**

3. **Wine Producer**

4. **Appellation status** (Classification) and Appellation (Region). This is the classification for non-DO wines in the autonomous region of Castilla-La Mancha, which includes the La Mancha DO and Jumilla DO.

Other notes: Since this area offer a wide range of wines, sniffing out the varietal(s) is challenging, but Tempranillo is the most common so it's your best guess here (and is correct).

1. **Wine Producer**

2. **Aging Designation** ("solera" refers to the Sherry aging methodology in which multiple vintages are mixed over time)

3. **The Type of Sherry**

4. **Name they have given this wine**

5. **The type of wine** (for those who don't know "Amontillado" is a type of Sherry)

6. **The city where it was produced**

Other notes: In this case, the Appellation (Jerez-Xérès-Sherry) and Appellation Classification (DO) are listed on the back label. No vintage is listed since this bottle combines multiple years.

CHAPTER 10:
SPANISH WINE + SPANISH CUISINE

A s if learning about and indulging in Spanish wines wasn't enjoyable enough, you can double your pleasure by adding food to the mix. But how should you go about pairing your dinner entrée or tapas with a glass (or bottle) of wine?

The basics are easy enough. Reds will generally pair best with powerful cheeses, red meats and other gamier fare. Whites often mix fabulously with seafood, milder cheeses and saltier foods. In short, the concept is that lighter wines can be overwhelmed by heartier dishes, while bigger, bolder red wines will help complement them.

Things get a little hairier when sauces enter the fray, but generally matching white wine with lighter sauces and red wine with darker sauces will create a tasty combo, with crossover dishes (sweet and spicy entrees, pink sauces, etc.) providing the perfect opportunity to experiment.

To increase the fun factor, try pairing your food with wine that hails from the same region of Spain. This is an awesome way to learn more about the country's geography, nudge you out of your comfort zone and make your wine-drinking adventures a little more interesting.

Given how much palates differ when it comes to wine alone, you can image the variance in opinion when foods enter the fray. Bottom line, you're going to have to dive in and see what you like. But take our word for it: This is "research" you're going to thoroughly enjoy.

To get you rolling, here's a starter guide to some classic Spanish foods and suggested pairings for you to consider:

FOOD ITEM	WHAT IS IT?	SUGGESTED PAIRINGS
Tortilla Española / Tortilla de Patatas	Potato and egg dish fried in olive oil, sometimes with chopped onion; can be served room temperature or cold	Verdejo, Tempranillo
Patatas bravas	Fried potatoes	Cava
Gazpacho	Cold vegetable soup	Fino or Manzanilla Sherry
Jamón Ibérico	Cured ham from free-roaming black pigs; the cheaper and more common Jamón Serrano is made from white pigs	Tempranillo, Amontillado Sherry, Cava
Croquetas	Tubes of béchamel sauce encased in fried breadcrumbs with some combo of ham, cheese, potato and fish; recipe changes based on region	Cava
Albóndigas	Spanish meatballs	Tempranillo, Garnacha, Manzanilla Sherry

Gambas al ajillo	Prawns fried with garlic and often flavored with paprika, lemon juice, parsley and chili	Albariño, Godello
Empanada	Savory "pie" with some combo of pork, chorizo, tuna, sardines, peppers, potatoes and tomatoes slow-cooked in onion sauce within bread	Mencía
Pimientos de Padrón	Small green peppers fried in olive oil and dusted with coarse sea salt	Albariño, Fino Sherry
Chorizo	Spanish sausage	Monastrell, Garnacha
Paella	Classic Spanish rice dish with saffron, chicken, rabbit, chorizo and/or seafood	Macabeo, Tempranillo, Monastrell, Bobal, Fino Sherry, Oloroso Sherry
Fabada	Spanish stew with beans, chorizo, pork belly, bacon and morcilla/blood sausage	Mencía
Pisto	Spanish version of ratatouille with tomatoes, peppers, zucchini, onion, garlic	La Mancha Tempranillo
Cochinillo asado	Roast suckling pig	Ribera del Duero Tinto Fino (Tempranillo)
Bacalao	Salt cod served with pil-pil sauce	Txakoli
Pulpo a La Gallega	Boiled octopus, often with paprika, salt and olive oil	Verdejo, Godello

CHAPTER 11:
READING A SPANISH RESTAURANT WINE LIST

W hen you're dropping some coin on a meal out, you want to enjoy the experience, not stress out about what wine to select. Yet that's exactly how many of us spend the first few minutes of a dining experience, poring over a wine list that can be overwhelming if not intimidating.

Sure, your waiter can often provide valuable insights to guide you, but his or her preferences may differ from yours, and you'll still want to narrow the options. With the clock ticking, what to do?

Part of the problem is often an unfamiliarity with the terms listed, especially when you're dealing with foreign wines and languages. Reading this book and learning the core Spanish regions and grapes will go a long way toward enhancing your experience.

Still, even the most seasoned wine drinkers are likely to see some stuff they're unfamiliar with. That's where today's diners have an edge: smartphones. Once you've zeroed in on a few interesting wines, you can do a quick smartphone search to learn more (and tap your waiter's knowledge to supplement).

CHAPTER 11: READING A SPANISH RESTAURANT WINE LIST

Our goal is for you to enjoy this part of the dining experience, feeling the excitement of recognizing grapes and regions as you peruse the list. The only tough part then? You can't try them all.

Let's take some sample listings culled from Spanish restaurants across the United States to get you started:

① **Cava, Brut, Poema, Spain NV**

Cava, Brut, "Anna de Codorniu", Codorniu, Spain NV

Cava, Brut, Juve y Camps, Spain 2011

Cava, Brut, "Reserva Heredad", Segura Viudas, Spain NV

1) Cava, Brut, Poema, Spain NV

Cava: The type of wine, in this case a sparkling wine made from the Macabeo (40%), Xarel·lo (40%) and Parellada (20%) grapes

Brut: Indicates the level of sweetness, in this case "brut," the driest tier

Poema: The winemaker

NV: Stands for "non-vintage," meaning the bottle is a blend from more than one year

Verdejo, Viura, Sauvignon Blanc

Viura, "Rioja Blanco", Muga, Rioja, Spain 2015

(2) **Viura, "Vetiver Blanco", Ontañón, Rioja, Spain 2014**

"Satinela", Marques de Caceres, Rioja, Spain 2013

2) Viura, "Vetiver Blanco", Ontañón, Rioja, Spain 2014

Viura: The grape/type of wine (known as "Macabeo" in parts of Spain)

Vetiver Blanco: The name of the wine

Ontañón: The winemaker

Rioja: The region

2014: The vintage

Xarel-lo, Albet i Noya, Penedes, Spain 2015

(3) **Txakoli, Bodegas Txakoli Txomin Etxaniz, Getariako, Spain 2015**

Hondarribi Zuri, Hondarribi Beltza

"Vina Esmeralda", Torres, Catalunya, Spain 2014

3) Txakoli, Bodegas Txakoli Txomin Etxaniz, Getariako, Spain 2015

Txakoli: The type of wine, in this case a blend of Hondarrabi Zuri and Hondarrabi Beltza

Bodegas Txakoli: Used in conjunction with the winemaker's name, meaning "Txakoli wine cellar"

Txomin Etxaniz: The winemaker

Getariako: The region (also known as "Getaria", "Getariako Txakolina")

2015: The vintage

Albariño, Paco & Lola, Rias Baixas, Spain 2014

Albariño, Licia, Rias Baixas, Spain 2015

(4) **Albariño, Don Olegario, Rias Baixas, Spain 2015**

Albariño, Pazo san Mauro, Rias Baixas, Spain 2015

4) Albariño, Don Olegario, Rías Baixas, Spain 2015

Albariño: The type of grape

Don Olegario: The winemaker

Rías Baixas: The region

2015: The vintage

Tempranillo, Volver, La Mancha, Spain 2013

Tempranillo, Entre Suelos, Spain 2014

Tempranillo, Tridente, Spain 2013

(5) **Tempranillo, "Gran Reserva", Anciano, Valdepeñas, Spain 2005**

5) Tempranillo, "Gran Reserva," Anciano, Valdepeñas, Spain 2005

Tempranillo: The grape

Gran Reserva: The aging designation, in this case indicating the wine
has aged a minimum of five years

Anciano: The name of the wine

Valdepeñas: The region, in this case a small one in southern Spain
that's mostly surrounded by the La Mancha DO

2005: The vintage, which has been rated "very good" by the
Valdepeñas DO

⑥ **Rioja, "Reserva", Campo Viejo, Spain 2010**

Rioja, "Reserva", Dinastia Vivanco, Spain 2010

Rioja, "Gran Reserva", Faustino I, Spain 2001

Rioja, "Gran Reserva", Campo Viejo, Spain 2010

6) Rioja, "Reserva", Campo Viejo, Spain 2010

Rioja: The region

Reserva: The aging designation, in this case indicating the wine
has been aged for a minimum of one year in oak and
two years in the bottle

Campo Viejo: The winemaker

2010: The vintage, in this case an excellent year for Spanish wine

Monastrell, Honoro Vera, Spain 2015

Monastrell, Tarima Organic, Alicante, Spain 2014

Garnacha, Vina Borgia, Campo de Borja, Spain 2015

⑦ **Garnacha, "Old Vine," El Chaparral de Vega Sindoa,
Navarra, Spain 2014**

**7) Garnacha, "Old Vine", El Chaparral de Vega Sindoa, Navarra,
Spain 2014**

Garnacha: The grape/type of wine

"Old Vine": The age of the vines, in this case, 70-100 years old

El Chaparral: The name of the wine

Vega Sindoa: The winemaker

Navarra: The region

2014: The vintage

Priorat, "Mas Mallola," Marco Abella, Spain 2008

⑧ **Priorat, "Clos del Mas," Pinord, Spain 2014**

"Borsao Berola," Bodegas Borsao, Campo de Borja, Spain 2013

"Can Blau," Cellers Can Blau, Montsant, Spain 2014

8) Priorat, "Clos del Mas", Pinord, Spain 2014

Priorat: The region

Clos del Mas: The name of the wine, in this case a blend of Cabernet Sauvignon, Cariñena and Garnacha

Pinord: The winemaker

2014: The vintage

Remember: Every wine list is going to be formatted differently. Some will be well-organized and make your decoding easy, while others will be a cluttered mess and omit key details that make it tougher to understand what you're looking at. If the restaurant you're going to posts its wine list online, consider taking a peek before you go so you can do some advanced sleuthing.

Beyond that, take a deep breath and have fun. One way or another, you're going to have a glass of Spanish wine in front of you within a few minutes, and that's a good thing.

CHAPTER 12:
LA CONCLUSIÓN

Whew. Hopefully you learned a lot on the previous pages, and it wasn't too much to absorb — wine consumption aside, of course. Fortunately, the "hard" part is over. The fun part, and the easy part, comes next: tasting and exploring more Spanish wines.

We've given you plenty of places to start. You'll definitely want to hunt for the wines we list in Chapter 8, and don't sweat the vintages. Just buy whatever you see and build your knowledge from there. If you score and see two of the same wine from different vintages, buy them both and open them together to note the differences.

Follow wineries on Instagram. Take pictures of the wine labels you enjoy. Write down your own tasting notes (writing notes helps you remember the wines better).

Wine is an exploration. A journey. A fun one, like collecting baseball cards for adults, complete with similar obsessions about climate control, storage amenities and how to best organize your collection.

Don't be afraid to ask questions, whether to your sommelier, wine shop owner or nerdy wine friends. You didn't learn any of this in school — at least, we hope not. It can only be gleaned through palate-building experiences, and hopefully we've inspired and set a nice backdrop to send you off on this adventure.

"If there were only one truth, you couldn't paint a hundred canvases on the same theme," said the legendary Spanish artist Pablo Picasso. True, ol' Pablo was talking about painting, but the same tenets apply to the wine world, where you'll find distinct wines originating from the same regions and grapes. Go out there, pull a few corks and discover your own favorite masterworks of the wine world!

APPENDIX I:

SANGRIA

When it comes to Spanish wine, there's no shortage of opinions about sangria. To some, it's one of the greatest Spanish inventions, a tantalizing mixture of wine and fruit with judicious dashes of liquor, juice, soda and spices. To others, it's a vile concoction often employed to make money off silly tourists.

As you've probably guessed if you've read this far, we're not a very judgmental bunch when it comes to people's wine preferences, so we weigh in on the former side of the debate: Sangria is downright delicious, especially on a hot summer day, and a perfectly acceptable addition to your wine-drinking arsenal.

A (VERY) BRIEF HISTORY OF SANGRIA

The origins of sangria are murkier than the syrups some restaurants use to create a low-budget version of this libation. Some sources say it dates back hundreds of years, with high-society Europeans enjoying red wine punch at their fancy parties. Others put its origins in medieval times. And a few even date it back to ancient Roman times, when the parched conquerors would experiment with vino in an effort to quench their thirst.

While sangria's birthdate may be tough to pinpoint, most experts agree that the modern-day sangria phenomenon was uncorked when it was "introduced" to U.S. audiences at the 1964 World Fair in New York City. Since then, thousands of variations of sangria have emerged.

SO, WHAT SHOULD YOU PUT IN THIS SHIZZLE?

Crafting the perfect sangria is largely a matter of personal preference, but to help guide you toward that goal, let's take a run through the ingredients often – and sometimes, not so often – found in sangria:

Wine: Your critical foundation. Red wine is the classic choice here, with "sangria" translating to "bleeding" in Spanish. Today, it remains by far the most common base in Spain.

With apologies to purists, though, white wine and rosé sangria variations have proliferated in recent years. If you're looking for some spritz but don't want to add soda water, a Cava-based version is also an option.

Fruit: Common additions include strawberries, blackberries, blueberries, raspberries, apples, pears, grapes, peaches, pineapple, oranges, lemons and limes.

If that's not enough options for you, more experimental versions sometimes include mango, cranberries, currants, watermelon, plums, lychees, cucumber (veggies!) and jalapenos (pain!). For the culinary-inclined, grilling the fruit can add flavor and aesthetics.

Liquor: Whether to balance the fruit's sweetness or give the sangria some extra bite, a splash (or more) of liquor is often added to the concoction. Brandy is the classic choice here, with other potential additions/alternatives including rum, triple sec (e.g., Cointreau) and Grand Marnier.

Less frequent options include vodka, gin and bourbon, with really offbeat selections ranging from sake, Campari and Black Haus to elderflower and Maraschino liqueurs. Hell, we're pretty sure that someone out there has made sangria with Jägermeister (though we wouldn't recommend it).

Soda Water: Sometimes added shortly before serving to give sangria that extra-festive fizz and up the refreshment factor. Depending on preference, ginger ale or a lemon-lime soda is occasionally subbed in here.

Juice: Though a less frequent addition, some will add incorporate lemon, orange, grape or pineapple juices to provide flavor and sweetness. If you want to get a little crazier, guava, cranberry and pomegranate juices are options, or you can mix in some pear or apricot nectar.

Sugar: A necessary addition for those with a sweet tooth. For the gourmet, "simple syrup" is sometimes used for similar purposes. Honey and brown sugar are other alternatives.

Spices: Gastronomes more advanced in their sangria studies sometimes experiment with incorporating herbs and spices such as basil, sage, mint, cinnamon and allspice. For those looking for some heat to balance the sweet, cayenne or crushed red pepper is another option.

5 TIPS FOR A STELLAR SANGRIA

As you can see, there's no shortage of possibilities when it comes to sangria. And let's face it, when it comes to sangria, the first rule is that there are no rules. Nonetheless, to help you cut through the chaos, here are some quick tips.

1) Don't go too cheap.

A common sentiment is that since you're mixing a bunch of stuff with the wine, you won't taste it anyway, so why not go with the cheapest bottle you can find? We encourage you to approach sangria as you would a mixed drink. In other words, better ingredients are going to make a superior beverage.

So while you aren't going to experience the nuances of a wine that would justify a high-end price tag, consider opting for a lower mid-range bottle. And for authenticity, we of course recommend keeping it Spanish. Tempranillo and Garnacha are classic choices that are tough to go wrong with.

2) Keep it simple.

Just because there are dozens of ingredients to choose from doesn't mean you can (or should) go nuts. Much like the best European cuisine, the finest sangria often comes from the simplest recipes.

Put another way, using fewer ingredients allows you to appreciate the flavors more. To continue the mixed drink analogy, a Long Island iced tea might go down smooth, but leave you without an appreciation for the ingredients and flavors within (not to mention a nasty hangover). Especially when you're starting out, consider using five or so ingredients as a good baseline.

3) Choose your fruit wisely.

You've read a lot in this book about the various fruit aromas and tastes that different wines can impart. So, why not use the fruit in your sangria to complement the fruits in your wine? For example, if you're using Garnacha as your base, you might select blackberries, blueberries and cherries, while a Verdejo-based white sangria might be matched with apples, peaches and melon.

Alternatively, you could take a cue from the Spaniards and use whatever fruit is in season. Fresh, ripe fruit is really going to take that sangria up a notch, delivering more flavor and remaining firmer as it marinates.

Any way you "slice" it, though, don't fret: Fruit soaked in wine is always going to be tasty, so it's tough to go wrong. Which brings us to our next point …

4) Give it some time to chill.

How long should you let your sangria marinate? It's a matter of endless debate, since added time gives the flavors more opportunity to mingle, but eventually can turn that wine to vinegar.

We've found that 12 hours is a nice sweet spot, delivering plenty of flavor without the fruit getting too gnarly or weirdness setting in. So, if you're prepping for an evening gathering, mixing first thing in the morning would help you hit that perfect point, whereas if you're imbibing for breakfast or brunch (don't judge us!), prepping right before bedtime should be the ticket.

Regardless, we'd recommend at least three hours to sit, and we'd proceed cautiously with going beyond 24. (Though to be honest and fair, we've indulged in several-days-old sangria and lived to tell about it – and even enjoy it.)

A final tip: While refrigerated, put a lid on your container or wrap it up in plastic wrap to keep the goodness in and oxygen out.

5) Avoid premixed sangria.
In today's go-go-go world, it can be tempting to purchase an already prepared bottle, add ice and drink. And while we appreciate that desperate times may call for desperate measures, we'd encourage you to choose differently.

For starters, who knows what's in that bottle? Part of the fun of sangria is using fresh, delectable ingredients, and it's anyone's guess what syrups, preservatives and chemicals are in those premixed bottles. (Likewise, this is why you should proceed with caution when ordering sangria at a restaurant.)

So, what to do when time is short? Even if you're looking at 90 minutes until go time, you can still prep a solid sangria – 30 minutes to mix, 60 to chill, then serve and continue marinating while you hang.

Working with less than an hour? Quickly pureeing or mashing up some of the fruit can help impart that flavor goodness on a short timetable. Also, this is where employing (or going heavier on) fruit juice options can come in handy.

THE FINAL WORD ON SANGRIA

As with your wine-drinking adventures, much of the fun of sangria is in the endless experimentation. Play around with different combinations and see what you like best. And please, share those recipes with us when you settle on a new killer concoction!

APPENDIX II:
CALIMOCHO

At least one website we've come across described Calimocho ("kah-lee-MOH-choh") as being drank by two types of Spaniards: students and metalheads. That might seem off-putting to some, but since we often like to think we're 20 years old and listen to head-banging music, it put smiles on our faces.

And it makes sense, since our first exposure to this exotic elixir came from college buddies returning from study-abroad programs. We'd listen wide-eyed as they told tales of drinking this unholy mix of Coke and red wine in liter bars in Spain.

Still, you don't have to be a teenager – or have an appreciation for Metallica and Megadeth – to enjoy Calimocho ("Kalimotxo" in Basque). But it does beg the question: Why would any self-respecting wine drinker ever, EVER mix our favorite libation with a cola product?

We're glad you asked. For one thing, there's nothing to take the starch out of a stuffy wine-drinking outing like popping a few cubes into a glass of red and pouring some Coke into it. That'll get the conversation started!

Furthermore, on those oh-my-god-I'm-going-to-die-of-the-heat days, when a red wine sounds about as appealing as drinking a glass of steaming hot coffee and you've already cycled through seven straight days of whites, firing up a Calimocho can break up the monotony and provide the refreshment you need.

Or, picture this: You're prepping to go out on a muggy summer night and feeling sluggish when you spot a neglected bottle of previously opened red in your fridge. Hmm. Perfect timing for a Calimocho – you can still get some use out of that bottle while the Coke provides a welcome jolt of energy as you're socializing Spanish-style into the wee hours of the night.

Finally, Calimocho can also serve as an alternative beverage for those guests who claim not to like wine. We know, it's hard to fathom, but they do exist.

Enough justification (as if any was needed), let's talk prep. Dialing up some Calimocho couldn't be easier. Grab a cocktail glass, pop in some ice cubes, and pull out a budget-friendly bottle of red (that $5 bottle of Tempranillo from Trader Joe's will do just fine here). Pour to roughly the halfway point, then fill the rest of the way with Coke – a 50/50 mix is the standard.

Congrats, you've just mixed a Calimocho. And whether you decide it's shockingly tasty or as noxious as you imagined, you've gone to a place few wine drinkers venture to. Rock on!

ACKNOWLEDGEMENTS

Andrew

I'd to thank Ryan for his excellent editing skills and ability to take my random thoughts and notes that were influenced at times by a little too much wine, and make them easy to digest and a lot more fun for readers. I'd also like to thank everyone who tasted and enjoyed so many of these Spanish wines with me over the last 12 months, and who understood when I needed to run off and write notes about them in the middle of hanging out. And finally, I'd like to thank my wife and family for providing the necessary time, amid a hectic schedule, for me to be able to focus on and write this book.

Ryan

First, a big shout-out to Andrew for bringing his vast wine knowledge and writing skills to the table and patiently answering my wine terminology questions. Second, thanks to my wife Vanessa for tirelessly assisting with my "research" and sharing many amazing Spanish wines with me – and admittedly, a few that were less than amazing. To my parents Ron and Rosemarie, thank you for encouraging me to explore other cultures and helping review this book. And last but certainly not least, cheers to my kids Marisa and Daniela for their boundless enthusiasm and unsolicited feedback ("Dad, are you ever going to write a book about something besides wine?").

Many other family members provided valuable assistance and support, so a roll call is in order: Emily (Spanish language expert extraordinaire), Luther (generous supplier of Spanish wine), Erin (skilled editing specialist), Clark (purveyor of beer), A.J. (maker of tasty paella) and Allison (companion on my first foray into Spain many years ago) … thank you, thank you!

And to DeFrank, Pittman and Clancy, much love for introducing me to the wonders of Calimocho.

Andrew and Ryan would also like to thank Karrie Gawron for her beautiful book design and tireless work in formatting every last detail with us. This book wouldn't be the same without her.

ABOUT THE AUTHORS

Andrew Cullen has authored and co-authored four nonfiction books about wine including *"Around the Wine World in 40 Pages," "Decoding French Wine: A Beginner's Guide to Enjoying the Fruits of the French Terroir,"* and *"Decoding Italian Wine: A Beginner's Guide to Enjoying the Grapes, Regions, Practices and Culture of the 'Land of Wine.'"* He has published two works of Fiction, *"The Callisto Symphony"* (2015) and *"A Gentle Slaughter of the Perfect Kind"* (2017).

He is a digital marketer for a global 100 brand and the founder of the Underside Publishing Co. (TheUnderSide.com), which has produced several websites including CostcoWineBlog.com. His writing and websites have been featured in the Wall Street Journal, Consumer Reports. The Daily Meal, HuffPost, CNN Money and CBS Marketwatch.

Ryan McNally has co-authored two books, including *Decoding Italian Wine*. He is a product marketing manager for a leading B2B software company and has written for dozens of magazines and websites on topics including music, sports and film.

Made in the USA
Coppell, TX
09 June 2020

27429337R00069